GOOD
DATES
GONE BAD

Volume 1

A book of short disastrous dating stories

by Lee Valentina

Good Dates Gone Bad
Volume 1

By Lee Valentina

Order this book online at www.trafford.com
or email orders@trafford.com

Most Trafford titles are also available at major online book retailers.

Print information available on the last page.

ISBN: 978-1-4669-0983-0 (sc)
ISBN: 978-1-4669-0985-4 (hc)
ISBN: 978-1-4669-0984-7 (e)

Library of Congress Control Number: 2011963401

Trafford rev. 03/28/2024

www.trafford.com
North America & international
toll-free: 844-688-6899 (USA & Canada)
fax: 812 355 4082

"This book is dedicated to all the Single People in the World, who believe that their special someone still exists. I know mine does. And he knows who he is."

-Lee Valentina

"The Dream"

Alone in my room my restless bed awaits

Bringing dreams and smiles so real,

So real, but lasting only for a moment

Not nearly long enough but to remember

And awakening brings frustration

Of a dream that cannot last.

The smile that slowly wakes me

As I sense you near,

Warms me like nothing I have ever felt before.

My heart is pounding faster with each smile

And I know it's you.

—Lee Valentina

PREFACE

After encountering many "Good Dates Gone Bad" of my own, and hearing many experiences similar to mine from my friends, I decided to collaborate the stories into this book. I noticed that several of my friends felt both embarrassed and humiliated having to recount their dating disaster, so my focus of sharing these anonymous stories with others would be an encouraging word, knowing that there truly are worse dates to be had, and that others could survive another dating experience.

After all, we are all similar in that we date to avoid being alone. Some of us seek to have children by a certain age and, as we near that time frame, we begin seeking both egg and sperm donors, knowing it is a bad idea or method of dating. We go on dating sites like Match dot com, E-Harmony dot com, even MySpace dot com, much to our exhaustion and disappointment. But when it comes right down to it, we all seek to find another person, special enough to share our lives. Unfortunately, we have to kiss a lot of frogs or weed through the trenches to find that special someone, and it can take years before we find someone compatible to our standards. And so we date, even when our better judgment is against us, and we get set up with people totally not our type, thinking maybe if we approach dating at a different angle we might find our true love. In keeping things light and to realize that dating is a must for singles, we must also see the humor in our dating experiences, and to keep putting one foot in front of the other, hoping we will find "The One" that ends our Good Dates Gone Bad. I hope this book will enlighten you, the reader, so you can recount a story or two with your friends when there is a funny story that needs to be told. Because, after all, dating is supposed to be fun, but ends up being funny!

ACKNOWLEDGMENTS

I would like to begin by expressing my sincerest gratitude to those who, although they are to remain anonymous, donated their stories to this book, in hopes of encouraging others of a worse dating situation. I thank my parents, who put up with me while I tried to explain to them my passion behind this book, barely able to recite any stories as they were in general rated R. My siblings who laughed at my mishaps, but donated some stories of their own, which made family gatherings even more bearable. My friends in Florida, Georgia, and New Mexico who believed in me and donated stories of their own, giving us all a good hearty laugh at our own dating disasters. To God, who has impressed upon me all this time that there was a different calling to my life, one unlike anything I could have ever imagined, in writing this book and creating things all by myself.

I am grateful for those in my life who encourage me to go out on my own to find my own light. To those in random coffee shops who overheard my laughter in editing this book, not realizing how funny the story was, and enlightening me with some stories of their own. For everyone who supported my dream and passion to complete this book, encouraging me to keep pressing forward, to not give up and to continue writing. Also, a great big "Thank You" goes out to those at Horse and

Angel in Albuquerque for allowing me to use their watering hole as a back drop for the cover of my book. I appreciate all that I have learned through writing, as this is my first publication, and I intend on writing another volume, hoping that all can benefit from these disastrous dating experiences as I have.

1

"It Happens"
(A Man's Story)

He got up the nerve to ask out this girl from the gym, and took her to a very nice dinner. After drinking a few bottles of Merlot, they decided to go back to her place. From the moment they walked into her house, the passion grew stronger between them, so she led him to her bedroom upstairs. Immediately, she lit candles and removed her dress. He knew it would be a night to remember, so he prepped himself mentally for a long night of gratuitous lovemaking. Once the deed was done, and a few hours had passed, he relaxed on her bed as she got up to take a shower.

He heard the cascading water running in the shower and lay in bed blissfully gloating on his recent achievements. A smile creeps across his face and he is content. As he relaxed, he let out a juicy fart, but to his surprise, he realized he had defecated all over the bed. Mortified at what just happened, he jumped up and quickly removed the designer 800 count, Egyptian sheets from the bed and proceeded to search the house for the laundry room. He had never been in her house before and knew the laundry room could be anywhere. After opening numerous doors, only to be disappointed in his rapid search, he finally found the washing machine. Yanking open the lid to the washer, he found a load of clean but wet clothes inside. Next, he frantically opened the dryer, hoping he could put the clean clothes inside, but found a load of clean and dry clothes inside. Not daring to set down the soiled sheets he carried in his arms, he thought of Plan B: the garbage can out front! Listening for water running, he felt confident in making the mad dash outside for the garbage can, so he opened the front door and took off around the side of the house. After reaching the garbage can, he placed the sheets inside. As he closed the garbage can lid, he had the strangest realization that he was not wearing any clothes! Evidentially, his mind was so preoccupied with the "clean up" rather than getting himself dressed appropriately, as if anything about the past ten minutes were deemed as such. Quickly, he thought of another plan and headed for the front door, only to find that the door had one of those side panel locks that allows you to open from the inside but is actually locked on the outside. Thankfully, it was approximately eleven o'clock in the evening and there weren't any cars on the street. It seemed as if to be a quiet enough night and no one appeared to be in their driveways to see him, so he felt secure in his nudity. Unsure of what to do out of sheer desperation, he ran into the bushes and left her house. His friend's house was just a few blocks away, so without any further thought, he ran through the neighboring yards until he arrived naked, completely out of breath, and knocking loudly on his friend's front door.

Irritated, his friend flung open his front door, "Dude, what the hell is going on?" "Man, you wouldn't believe what just happened to me!" he said out of breath and sweating. "Well, I wondered how your date was going but damn, what happened?! And what happened to your clothes, man?"

Standing in the doorway, with the front porch light revealing his naked and shit-stained ass to all who happened to notice, he proceeded to tell him all the ignorance of the last hour, while slowly inching his way into his home and out of the light. His friend covered his nose and mouth with his hand and said, "Really, dude, you smell like ass, and I can't take it!" Bowing his head in shame, he begged for him to let him shower, borrow some clothes, and bum a ride home. The poor girl never contacted him, probably out of anger for being left after hooking up the first night and surely wondering what happened to her sheets! Unfortunately for him, he didn't have the heart or stomach to contact her, despite the fact that she had his cell phone, keys, and clothes. Fortunately for him, he never saw her again.

2

"MESSED UP MAN"
(A Woman's Story)

After recent college graduation, she was hired on by a major department store in Atlanta. Her friend's younger brother was also moving there, and they decided to become roommates. They had never met until the move-in date, so they had a lot of catching up to do as new friends. Both of them were considered above average in the appearance department and very social, which made it easy to go out to the area clubs and enjoy a cocktail, vowing to the inevitable title of "Wing Man". One night they decided to go out in Buckhead, a hot spot with numerous bars and clubs, to have a cocktail. They had been standing by the bar, sipping adult beverages, and people watching. After about thirty minutes, a very handsome devil approached her, brazen as he couldn't possibly have known her relationship with her roommate. He was very interested in getting to know her, obviously not caring if she was with the man standing beside her. After the introductions, he offered to take her out and asked if they could exchange phone numbers. At the time, she was twenty-seven and he confided that he was forty-two, so she thought she might have been pushing it a bit by contemplating a date with this man. He was so cute though, so she consented to offering her phone number in exchange for his, in hopes of arranging a second meeting.

He called her two nights later and they chatted for about an hour, planning a date for the upcoming Wednesday. He suggested, "Why don't you meet me at one of my favorite seafood restaurants, being that you are from Florida and all". She replied, "That sounds great! What's the name of the restaurant?" assuming he knew a good seafood restaurant from a bad one. He went on to say, "It's called Joe's and I know you will love it! By the way, I live in Kennesaw, so it may be a bit of a drive for you, but during rush hour traffic, it will be a drive for either one of us. You don't mind that I'm not coming to pick you up, do you?" After a moments pause, she responded, "No, no, don't be silly, it's fine. I suppose I could meet you there", not realizing how far away the restaurant was from her nine-to-five job in Buckhead. So, after work on Wednesday, she drove in hellish, Atlanta rush hour traffic only to arrive one hour and fifteen minutes later in the parking lot of a place called "Joe's Crab Shack". She was given the location of the restaurant from a coworker, who, snickering, said, "Yeah, it's a great seafood restaurant, you are going to love it!" She immediately phoned him and inquired, "Am I at the correct location, I mean, this just doesn't seem like the place you had described?" As she feared his reply, he said, "Yeah, you're in the right place. In fact, I'm about to pull into the parking lot right now. See you inside, ok!" To paint the scene, she was wearing her retail management garb, twin sweater set, trousers, loafers, as she walked into the noisy, unsophisticated restaurant, where kids are running around like monkeys, and the guys beer guts which began at their sternums. They hadn't seen their own packages in quite some time.

Disgusted at his choice of establishment, but willing to try new things and to just go with the flow, she found an empty picnic table, with the classic plastic red and white checkered table cloth, throwing one leg over the bench seat. Straddling, she was approached by a female server and she immediately ordered a Bud Light, noticing the server's bad teeth. "This is going to be AWESOME", she sighed and mumbled under her breath. Just then, he walked through the tattered front doors, looking handsome in his navy sports coat, jeans, loafers, bearing a long-stemmed red rose, and holding what appeared to be a photo album. They were both overdressed and she was feeling a bit out of place, as she was not proudly sporting one of the "Joe's Crab Shack" bibs that seemed to be so popular in the establishment!

He approached her with a "Hey, good to see you again", and he kissed her cheek, presenting her with the rose. She greeted him with a smile and said, "Yes, you too, and thank you for the rose, you really shouldn't have", questioning the formality of his presentation, and simultaneously, his lack of taste in a quality restaurant. The server approached bringing her bottled beer, leg was still straddling the seat as if she could care less, and he said, "Hey, I'll have the same thing she's having". He smiled and presented his photo album, as if to not waste any time in showing her his past. Lamenting, he took her through his long-haired hippy days, upon which he took his time flipping through and explaining each picture. One picture was of his Harley Davidson motorcycle, another was his children, and when he arrived at a picture of his former wife, he paused. She looked at him and his eyes became teary. The server's timing was impeccable, as she brought over his beer. He thanked her with a quivering voice. "This awkward moment brought to you by Bud Light", she commercialized in her head, as if to make light of the situation and keep from cracking up from the humor of it all. She placed one arm around his shoulder to comfort him, encouraging him to continue as if the woman had passed onto the next life. After a long pause and several sniffles, he said, "I have to tell you something. My wife and I split because we were swingers and it ruined our marriage." Slowly removing her arm from around his shoulder, she just looked at him with disbelief. Tuning out his next sentences, she was unsure of what would come out of her mouth at that very moment, but knowing it was going to be critical, she tried desperately to bite her tongue. "What an idiot!" she thought to herself, hoping her thoughts weren't too loud for him to hear. She was unsuccessful because eventually, while he was in mid-sentence about some wild sexual encounter he had with another woman, she interrupted, "Why are you telling me this? Do you think this is a good thing to talk about on a first date?" Her voice was obviously annoyed and loud. Just as she thought about getting up to leave, he leaned over to her and tried to kiss her on the lips! Irritated at his behavior, and for driving all this way for this crap, she pulled away and stood up. Leaning towards him, she gave him a quick hug, and said, "We are going to be good friends, but that is all". Stunned and still crying, she left that man sitting there on the stupid picnic bench mulling over his bad decisions in life with a bottled beer and his pathetic photo album. She left without looking back, slamming her car door, and contemplating her drive-through dinner, "Ah, McDonald's sounds like a great idea", as she headed home. Thankfully, he never tried to contact her, which made her wonder what happened to the next girl he tried courting. And she made sure that the next time she was invited to dinner, she would Google it first!

3

"Crazy Bitch"
(A Man's Story)

He was out with his older brother, Tim, who loved the fact that the ladies were attracted to his younger brother's shyness, but inevitably would agree to go home with him. This night was different, as he was approached by an attractive woman while standing near the bar of a local hot spot in Atlanta. Her attempt at attaining his affections was to offer her business card with her cellular number written on the back, simply stating "Call me". He read the words out loud back to her, as if to question the request by a woman he had never even met. His face turned red and she added, "You're cute. Want to hang out sometime?" Then she jumped in before he could say a word, "I'm a crazy bitch, so if you think you can handle that, give me a call". Out of sheer shock and fear of upsetting her, he replied nervously, "Sure! I will call you!" And with that, she walked away with her friends and left the bar. At this point, his brother was elbowing his side, saying something stupid and boyish like, "Bro, she just gave you her number, way to go!" He didn't say much else about it because, well, there wasn't anything else to say about it, but he decided to give her a call in the next few days.

Getting up the nerve to contact this perfect stranger-woman, she happens to mention a friend's birthday party that is coming up while they spoke briefly on the phone and she asked, "I need to test you out, you know, to see how cool you are". "Uh, okay", was his only response as he was perplexed at how far this "test" would go. They agreed to meet at a local hotel bar, which was known for their charity events. This was one of those evening events that also happened to be the hostess' birthday party. He had to work late that day, and was stuck in traffic trying to make his appearance in a timely manner, but was late to the party. She left him a voice message around five o'clock in the evening to ask, "Hey, could you possibly bring some party favors with you to the party". He listened to the message, trying to decode her mysterious "party favor" request, but unfortunately could not locate any such treats as he was running so behind. As if he wasn't aware of his tardiness, she kept calling him, blowing up his phone with text messages too, informing him of the matter, "Where are you", "Did you forget about the party tonight", "I was counting on you to be my date", "I hope you brought some party favors because I'm dying here"! All of a sudden, he felt overwhelmed by her overtones that he realized what was to come from an evening with this woman. And it wasn't going to be pretty.

He found a parking spot, managed to pay the attendant, and rushed over to the hotel bar to meet her. She sees him and immediately begins waving frantically, as she pushes patrons and party guests over so she may greet him. Embarrassed, but managing a smile and a hug, he greeted her saying "Hey, good to see you". She exclaimed, "Damnit, you are so late, shit", as she grabbed hold of his hand, leading him towards her group of friends, who were evidently informed of his tardiness and giving him that certain look of disappointment. He knew he needed a drink for this one, a big one with Crown Royal written all over it so he excused himself from the group after being introduced, asked her if he could buy her a drink, which she assumed he was going to do, and he approached the bar. "Finally, a moment to stand still for once today", he thought, sipping his drink a few times before returning to her side. She seemed frustrated and manic at the same time, and it was very hard to follow her conversations. She also kept slapping her friends on the back and bugging them, as they would say loudly, "Stop, Kate, seriously, that hurts!"

Curious as to what her deal was, he boldly asked his date what was going on. Broaching the subject of the request of "party favors" as it was weighing heavily on his mind, he asked, "What did you want me to get for tonight anyway, I mean, I have no idea what your poison is". She leaned in to whisper, "You know, blow, or rolls, or maybe even heroin". Gasping and his jaw hanging, she calmly continued, "Yeah, I shot up before I came out tonight and it's finally wearing off, but the alcohol is kicking in so I should be fine, I just wanted to cover my ass". Unable to contain his surprise, he screamed, "Are you serious, I mean, you really shot up heroin tonight for our date, for this event? I mean, how could you do that?" She immediately grabbed his hand and said, as if to ignore his response, "Come on, by me another drink". He turned around and said, "No, thank you, but I believe this is my time to exit the building". He walked away from her, leaving her in a panic to keep him there, as if he were her only friend at the party. As he made his rounds to say good-bye to her friends, they all seemed to have the same question, "Hey, what is a nice guy like you doing with a crazy girl like her?" His only response was to say it was nice to meet them and that it was time for him to leave. And so he left, not even meeting the birthday girl or offering a donation to the charity. After being there for thirty minutes in agony, he had learned what would be very valuable in a single man's dating life: never, ever, take a number from a woman in a dark bar, and if she tells you that she's crazy, believe her.

4

"LOST IN SPACE"
(A Woman's Story)

It was their first date, really, after meeting in a bar in Midtown, Atlanta. They spent most of the night talking and kissing in a dark corner at the club, and decided to resume their make-out session at his place, a few nights later. Upon reaching his apartment, she was a little nervous, but confident in her sexual abilities that it would be a good experience. He opened his apartment door and greeted her with a kiss and a smile.

They immediately connected through a toast with a cocktail of vodka and tonic, no lime of course, and made their way to his bedroom. On his bedside table lay a silver bullet masturbation device, which she assumed he would be using on her, and she noticed it didn't have a string. She was glad to see it was not a nine-inch, plastic dildo on a chain saw. He began to kiss her neck and then her lips and it just felt so good; she didn't want to ask him to stop. He slowly reached for her glass and set it down on his dresser, while his other hand removed her tank top and threw it across the room as if to say, "Here we go!" It was summer and the room was steamy! They began touching each other erotically, and she went along with it, assuming things would heat up and she would get a few orgasms before penetration. He led her over to his California King mattress and began dry humping her crotch, as if to say, "Let's get it on, Baby!" She was very excited and about to ask him to help her remove her pants when she felt his hand brush past her crotch. He was unzipping his own pants and leaving her pants on! Puzzled of such a move, she realized his strong arms then wrapped around her and flipped her over on top of him. All along, neither one of them are talking to each other, just engrossed in one another's tongue and lips, and hips and ass. She was wondering where all of this was going and reached to unzip her own jeans, as he interrupted her movement, saying, "Wait, I want you to use this on me first". She looked down at his hand, which bore the silver bullet from his nightstand. She replied in confusion, "You want me to use this on you? Okay, whatever works". He slowly removed his boxer briefs, as if to tease her and remind her that he will be the only one naked. His boyish smile, bordering on homosexuality at this point, precluded his next request, "I want you to fuck me in the ass with it". Astonished, but again intrigued, she agreed to his request, forgetting all about any requests of her own that she envisioned previously. At this point, her level of excitement came to a screeching halt.

As she longingly glanced up at the beads of sweat on her cocktail glass, wishing for a drink and a buzz to enhance this awkward moment, he reached for the warming lubricant on his bedside table and proceeded to pour it all over the silver bullet. It was really too much lubricant on such a small sex toy, but he was feeling a bit over-zealous. By now his erection was looking very appetizing but she knew he had other intentions. He jumped onto the bed and laid in a missionary position with his feet on the mattress. "This looks like a birthing position", she thought to herself. Not exactly confident of how to handle the slick object, she inserted it into his raised ass and began massaging his balls. She was watching him for a few moments but his eyes were closed and he was trying to get into the feeling without involving her, as she was merely the assistant in his pleasure plan. He was moaning and groaning and really enjoying it all, as she tried desperately to stay involved. She began to look around the room out of sheer boredom, when all of a sudden, he sucked the silver bullet into his ass, and she no longer had a grip of it. He didn't notice at first, but once he looked down at her as he was about to climax, she had both hands over her mouth, and she was trying very hard not to laugh out loud. "What's wrong?" he screamed, almost annoyed that her hysterical laughter broke his concentration. She shouted while pointing to his ass, "You sucked it in! It's up your ass!" Now a bit panicked, he screamed louder, "What?!" He immediately lifted up each leg by his knee and tried to push out the silver bullet, making every ungodly and disgusting sound imaginable. By now, she's trying to contain her laughter at the humor of this ridiculous scenario, and even feeling a little sorry for him too.

This is the moment that she was realizing the purpose of the missing string, typically attached to such a sex toy, probably to keep this exact situation from occurring. The more she laughed, the more upset he became, and he got off the bed and went into the bathroom, trying to push the silver bullet out while sitting on the toilet. Shaking her head, she thought, "This man has no shame", and he really asked for all of this in her opinion. That fact only made her laugh harder, bringing tears to her eyes. He opened the bathroom door slightly and peered around crying, "I can't believe you are laughing about this, I mean, I think I need to go to the hospital or something! Call an ambulance!" She went over to his dresser, picking up and finishing her watered-down cocktail, and said, "I think you will be okay. I think you are used to this. If anything, you will see it again in a few days". And with that, she located her tank top that was flung on the other side of the room, put it on, and wiped her slippery hands on his bedspread. Leaving him crying and moaning on his toilet, she made her escape. "How pathetic", she mumbled. Knowing now where that toy had been, she was very thankful he didn't try to use it on her. Next time, she will be sure to get to know a guy better before assuming that awkward position.

5

"LADIES CHOICE"
(A Man's Story)

He was a Freshman at Florida State University and just got out of a relationship with a girl named Stacey. Stacey was supposed to be so classy and mature. At the time, he was nineteen and she was the older woman, aged twenty-four. They both thought that the age difference between them was steamy, but the relationship inevitably ended after only three months of passion. She was the one to end the courtship and blew him off. His pride was crushed and for the first time, he was actually upset due to the breakup. Stacey stopped taking his phone calls and would say things like, "He's stalking me" to her friends, which he just couldn't believe to be true. Eventually, after two agonizing weeks of being alone, he met this girl named Libby, who was very exotic and gorgeous. He and Libby were pretty hot and heavy for about two months, but he came to realize how pretentious she was, noticing a lot of red flags in the first few weeks, so he wanted out of the relationship. As they were coming to the end of their courtship, she grew more comfortable with their friendship, and began to share stories with him about her past marriage, and her destructive behavior while driving. Being the cautious man that he was, he always elected to drive whenever they went out. Thus he was driving her brand new Mustang during the night in question.

The final evening of their friendship, they agreed to go out to Fat Tuesday's, and he excused himself to use the restroom shortly after entering the establishment. As he came out of the restroom, he witnessed Libby sitting at the bar, conspicuously flirting with his ex-girlfriend, Stacey! He knew Libby was bisexual, but he had never seen her in action. She had her arm around Stacey's waist, whispering in her ear, laughing out loud, and he had never felt more awkward or in shock than at that very moment. He approached them to see if they would break away, knowing he used to date both of them, but they just ignored him. Fuming out of humiliation, he ordered a shot of tequila and continued to stand nearby, hoping they would eventually say something out of recognition. After ten agonizing minutes, they got up, still laughing about who knows what, and walked out of Fat Tuesdays, leaving him standing at the bar by himself, feeling stupid and rejected. It was a slap in the face! Not only did Stacey break up with him, but Libby was leaving him at the bar to go home with Stacey! He ordered another shot of tequila, this time ignoring the lime and salt, and did a quick scoping of the bar to see if there was anyone watching this horror in action. To his luck, no one was even looking in his direction so he made his exit, quickly to phone a friend to pick him up. He never heard from either of the women again. Lesson to be learned here was never date a bisexual, because they will screw you in the end, and not in a good way.

6

"PARTY HEARTY"
(A Woman's Story)

On Valentine's Day, she was invited to a Tesla and David Lee Roth concert in Albany, Georgia. Her date organized with a group of his friends to caravan to the show. She rode with her date, Shaun and his best friend, Colt, and realized she had not eaten dinner out of nervousness of their first date. One of the guys in the car brought weed and they drank cheap beer on the way to the show, growing very drunk and stoned. Once they pulled into the parking lot of the arena, Shaun walked with her, practically holding her up as she was very out of it. He then dragged her down to the front row and she began to feel lightheaded, drunk and ended up passing out due to the heat and loud music. About twenty minutes later, she woke up in Shaun's arms, as he had revived her from passing out and she vomited due to her head being dizzy. Embarrassed for being sick and passing out, she held his hand, searching for a sign that he was cool with the situation. He asked if she was okay and unsure if she should be honest, she replied, "Yes", so he grabbed her hand and hurriedly ran up the nearby stairs to get to the next level for a better view of Tesla. She passed out again at the top due to the heat. Unable to revive her again, Shaun had to carry her out to the outer ring of the stage and he let her sit still while he went to get her a drink to settle her stomach. They missed the entire second half of the show but she did see Tesla, well, some of the show anyway, but missed all of David Lee Roth!

Very disappointed and nauseated, she asked Shaun if they could leave and get some food. Turned out, no one had eaten before going to the show, so they headed to a nearby McDonald's. Evidently, this particular location was the hot spot after concerts and the place was slammed. She held in her hands some chicken nuggets and managed to eat three of them, only to discover that this meal would soon be seen again. She made it to the sidewalk outside of McDonald's and hurled all over the place. Thinking she would be okay and ready to enter the van, she only made it five miles and felt nauseated again. This time, she held the bag containing the remaining three chicken nuggets, and was instructed to puke into the bag, as if it would support her vomit. After doing so and listening to the others in the car become squeamish, she handed Shaun the disgusting bag of vomit and told him to throw it out the window. He had one arm around her, rubbing her back and one hand trying to roll down the window. She glanced over to see Colt's face as he expressed disgust with the slow dripping of her vomit which was now all over Shaun's clothes.

Colt had managed to pull his van over to the side of the road, and her good-natured date jumped out of the van just as the vomit was making way down his pants. Mortified, she put her head in her hands and waited for the sounds of disgust from everyone, but luckily everyone was reassuring and cool with the situation. Shaun kept saying, "It's okay, it's all good", and stripped off his jeans, threw them in a plastic bag in the back of Colt's van and jumped back into the van beside her, only wearing his underwear. She wasn't sure if she would hear from him again, and quickly said "Good-bye", as she was dropped off at her house. Turned out, she was invited out on a second date with Shaun and managed to date him for the next year and a half. Lesson learned that night was to eat something before going out on a date, because you never know what you will get into.

7

"Go Cat Go!"
(A Man's Story)

He and his girlfriend of two months were hanging out at her place all day one weekend having a great time. It was a perfect Saturday, the weather outside was gorgeous, and the air conditioning was kicking. They had decided to make dinner together and she already had all the fixings so they didn't even have to leave her house. The meal was amazing. She prepared veal parmesan and he made spinach salad and garlic bread, but while they were cooking, he was very distracted because she insisted on cooking in her bra and panties, which really turned him on. He managed to succeed in getting through dinner without attacking her during the process and as horny as she was making him, he encouraged her to sit on the couch with him to make-out.

She put on some chick flick, the name he could not recall, but what really caught his attention were her hands all over him. Afraid of a pop quiz after the movie by her asking typical questions like, "Didn't you like the part when the girl did this or that?" he decided to throw in the towel so to speak, closing his eyes while they were kissing. It was her fault he was missing the movie, if you ask him. Her tongue was licking him in places he could only smile about and he loved every minute of it. He motioned for them to move their passion into her bedroom and she smiled in agreement, as things were getting pretty hot and heavy at this point. After about ten minutes, they began having sex, but he reached his peak way too soon, due to the constant teasing he had experienced all day long, and not to exclude the tortuous dinner attire. So not to disappoint her, he headed south to keep her in the mood and to distract his urge to orgasm. Just as she was about to explode, her Persian cat purred and rubbed its fluffy and tantalizing tail up against his erection, which didn't help his struggle to contain himself. Her moans and groans didn't really help either. He tried desperately to keep his composure, with her every intoxicating moan and the damn cat's tail, but couldn't contain how erotic this moment of intimacy sustained. He almost felt bad that his girlfriend wasn't in on the experience. The cat's tail was teasing and taunting him to the point of no return!

Being the gentleman that he was, he notified her of his nearing orgasm but she just ignored him, hoping they would be in unison and continued to moan as if she were also near. He couldn't contain himself any longer. Releasing his fiery demons before she did, he was a little embarrassed realizing her experience was incomplete. Disappointed, she sat up and whined, "Baby, what happened, I was almost there, I mean, you can't go a little longer for me, please? I mean, I'm almost there!" He looked at her disappointed face and then down at his end of the bed, not finding the "mess" to which would have been the result of his orgasm. "Huh", he said out of surprise, as he looked curiously for the cat, then hearing it purring as it slowly slinked towards her on the bed and its fur was streaked wet.

As he shook his head in disbelief, almost laughing about the situation, his girlfriend noticed it simultaneously and shrieked, "I can't believe you came on my cat, how could you do that?" And with that, she jumped up and grabbed her cat, and ran into the bathroom, all the while coddling her cat and scrubbing its fur to rid of the "mess" he made. It was the cat's fault. Hell, it was his girlfriend's fault for teasing him all day and night. But to be honest, he was way too relaxed in his release to truly care what had happened. He dragged his ass out the door, never to date her again. Lesson learned, shove the damn cat away while you are making love to your woman no matter how erotic the tail may feel.

8

"THE LEG HUMPER"
(A Woman's Story)

She had met him out one night, while barhopping in Atlanta with her roommate, Jonathan. After a few brief phone conversations, she arranged for him to pick her up from her apartment and for her friends from college to meet her at Frankie's Pub, a local pool hall. Upon arriving at her front door, he was dressed in a white painter's outfit, admitting he had just come from work. A little embarrassed for her date but not wanting to discourage him at the beginning of the evening, she smiled and quickly grabbed her handbag from the kitchen counter, exiting her apartment, and they walked towards the parking lot. As they rounded the corner she noticed, in between breaths of nervously jabbering on about her day, that a giant white Ford truck was parked in the lot. She smiled and began to joke about it's presence as he said, "There she is, my Baby-Girl", pointing to the albino beast that she was about to shame, bearing the most embarrassing and largest set of tires. "How in the hell will I get in this thing", she thought to herself as he opened her door like a gentleman. Regretting her decision to wear her new Guess mini skirt and unsure of which panties she had on, he gave her a much needed boost into the passenger seat of the cab, only to comment, "Whoa, I've got the best view right now!" Giving him a look that could kill she murmured, "Damn, what in the hell did I do, consenting to a date with this hick". A few moments later, as he made his way around the monstrosity, he opened the driver's door, jumping into his seat. Afraid to ask if this truck was his work vehicle, she decided to keep her questions and opinions to herself and put her hand over her mouth, laughing under her breath, unsure of what the night had in store for her. He must have known what she was thinking as he laughed, "Sorry, I just got new tires and it's a little taller than before, I'm still getting used to it!" The worn company logo plastered on the side of "Baby-Girl" resembled a local company name she had seen before, and she tried to recall the position he held within the corporation to which he claimed was so gainfully employed.

As they drove down the road, she gave directions to the location of the bar while screaming over the loud muffler sound. As if to answer her thoughts he responded, "I just had the new muffler installed, doesn't it sound cool?" "Oh good Lord", she mumbled as she just looked at him questioning his taste. Thinking he would change the noise, he turned on his stereo which screamed Two Live Crew rap music, as if to confirm her thoughts that this guy was truly lost in the eighties. She gave him directions to Frankie's Pub with her index finger, only because he couldn't have heard a single word from her due to his bad music, repulsive bass, and extremely loud sound system kicking in the cab. She began to feel like a high school girl on a first date, not someone who had graduated from college and was career-minded, but that guy who attended community college and hasn't gotten around to graduating. As they neared their destination, he turned up the volume of his music even louder, and the windows began to rattle. "Now, this is high school", she found herself stating out loud while covering her ears with her hands, knowing full well he could have only read her lips due to the piercing sound and bad music from his truck. He deliberately circled the parking lot several times before settling on a spot that could accommodate his large vehicle, but more importantly to inform the other patrons in the parking lot that he was the one responsible for the bass.

Thoroughly mortified, she clumsily climbed out of the cab of his truck, only to flash all who cared to look, and moved quickly away from the truck to limit her association. They walked together, but not hand in hand, towards the door, and she located her friends inside almost immediately. Her gay friend, Jason, was appalled at the appearance of the truck from the front window, as she led him away for a moment to reveal her recent horror. "Shut up, it's the worst!" he exclaimed as they walked back laughing about the beginning of her evening and to locate her date. She almost couldn't believe how well her date was getting along with her friends, and began to loosen up and enjoy herself. As the night progressed, they played a few games of pool, talking mostly and getting to know one another. Her friends were all leaving as they had to work early the next morning, so they said their farewells and paid their tab, heading for his disaster of a vehicle.

After pulling into her apartment complex, she begged him to turn off the music so the neighbors would not complain and he obliged. As she climbed out of the seat again, he asked if he could use her bathroom before leaving. She said that he could and she proceeded to sit on the couch, turning on the television for background noise, as if her ears weren't ringing enough. Discovery Channel had a show on about beetles and she grew fascinated in the dark room, only illuminated by the television light, as the sounds of him utilizing the facilities were drowned out. Within minutes, not noticing that he had sat down beside her, he began kissing her neck and the kiss was so good that she just let it happen. They kissed for about five minutes when all of a sudden, throwing her back on the couch, he began dry humping her left thigh, as if it was the prime spot for sexual pleasure. "Whoa, hey, what are you doing?" she said in a low tone, not to upset him as she was now in a compromising position. This horny poodle bore a glazed look, as he was trying to get off on her leg, not caring if it were even satisfying to her, and would not stop despite her pleas. Unsure of how to disarm this horny toad, she asked him to stop while pushing on his chest, but he didn't pay any attention to her request as he was in mid-hump and nearing climax. After several attempts of tying to stop him from inevitable embarrassment, and actually reaching climax while wearing his clothes, she realized it was too late! He finished, right then and there, all the normal sounds from a man who has had a very satisfying orgasm, in his pants. Appalled and bearing a sore left thigh, she demanded he leave her apartment immediately. He looked lazily over at her, smiling as if to say, "Thank you", and left her apartment, never to contact her again, for which she was eternally grateful.

9

"ACCIDENTALLY YOURS"
(A Man's Story)

A guy was hosting a party at his house, which he shared with his older brother and another roommate. Everyone had a date for the party, except his date was the hottest girl in the house! Everything was cruising along just fine until she became very drunk and needed to rest, which he offered that she lay down upstairs on his bed until she felt like joining the party again. She agreed it would be the best thing, so she went upstairs and periodically he sent friends to check on her for safety purposes.

After a few hours, a friend of his walked into the kitchen to report that his date had gotten sick and had an apparent "accident", due to lovely odors emitting from his closed bedroom door. He immediately went upstairs to check on his date, whom was not lying on his bed, but rather resting on the floor, passed out, by the toilet. Evidentially, his date had simultaneously vomited and soiled her shorts. She literally got sick from both ends, which totally grossed him out, leaving him unsure of how to handle the situation alone.

He elected to involve his older brother who was hanging out in the basement entertainment room with friends, asking him to accompany him to his bedroom to assist with the debacle. The two men had to run water in the bathtub enough to get her washed off, and as they placed her in the tub, his brother struggled to remove her shorts and upon removal, the water became brown with feces, which completely disgusted them. As the older brother was gagging due to the stench, she suddenly opened her eyes, and looked questioning at her date as if to ask, "What are you doing? What is happening?" Freaked out at what she might be thinking, he said to her, "Its okay, you're okay! I'm just trying to get you cleaned up because you had an accident!" Her look of questioning haunted him, but he couldn't do anything else for her except get her cleaned up, placing her somewhere so that if another accident occurred, she would be alright.

The next morning, amidst the rubble of a humble keg party and early morning guests just heading home, he was washing dishes in the kitchen. His date made her way down to the kitchen where he was and tried to give him a "Good Morning" kiss, but he turned his cheek so she would plant one there. He was still disgusted from the previous evening, and could not seem to muster up much more than a smile and a "Good Morning" response. Confused at his reaction to her kiss, she left without saying a word, and went to church that morning. He never did tell her what happened the night before, during the party, or what everyone else knew had occurred. He just never called her again.

10

"Odorous Among Us"
(A Woman's Story)

She met him while working at the gym. He was a regular lunch time gym rat and totally hot. One of his coworkers approached her, Stacey, and was trying to gage her interest in him. Admitting he was attractive and appealing, she gave Stacey the "go ahead" for him to ask her out. That should have been a clue. Since that day, he came in on a daily basis, giving her "the eye" as she scanned his membership card. As the others led the way out of the gym and back to the office, he stopped by the counter and asked her for her phone number and added, "May I call you this evening?" She replied blushing, "Of course, I would like that." Later that night, he called just as she hoped and they arranged a date the upcoming weekend, offering him directions to her apartment so he would pick her up. Oddly, he didn't suggest a dinner date, but rather the Andretti Speedway in Roswell, which is a go cart venue with video games. A place for kids, really, but she figured if they were racing each other on go carts, they wouldn't have the pressure of talking so much, as he was incredibly shy about asking her out on his own.

He phoned her as he was approaching the house to announce himself, and she waited patiently near the door so not to keep him waiting, and also so that her kooky roommate would not presume he was there for her. Her roommate was the jealous and competitive type, which she couldn't quite understand when it came to being friends. As he rang the doorbell, she opened the door with a great big smile and offered him a hug. They left her apartment and walked down the corridor towards his glossy, light blue BMW. He was a manager of some sorts for World Com and made a nice living for himself. Giddiness overwhelmed her as his chivalry began to shine when he opened the car door for her. He blushed as he shut her car door, walking slowly towards his door. Pausing a moment, he opened his car door, climbing inside and bringing the worst odor along with him. He had obviously broken wind as he walked around the car and had hoped, she was sure, that the offensive odor would dissipate before he entered the car. The smell reminded her of those suffering from lactose intolerance. Her poker face was in full force as she tried not to wince and politely talked about random subjects, trying to suppress the urge to roll down her window, which would surely embarrass him. She kept thinking, "Why doesn't he roll down his window as a courtesy?"

Luckily, the ride to the go cart hangout was only five agonizing miles away, so she took slow steady breaths so not to literally inhale the stench. His blushing increased but his conversation did not, making the awkwardness of the situation all the more uncomfortable. They were off to a rocky start, but she was determined to survive this date, as she knew she would see him again at the gym. "Stacey is going to die laughing when she hears what he did", she screamed in her head. They arrived at Andretti's and she quickly bolted from the car, hoping she didn't seem too anxious to get out of the green cloud. Once inside, he suggested that they go upstairs to have a cocktail and talk for a bit before hitting the go carts, and she thought that a drink to smooth things over was a good idea. Excusing herself, she went to the ladies room to regroup. A few minutes later, she walked up the stairs to the bar where he was sitting and the bartender immediately caught her glance, giving her a slight wince, and she knew exactly what to expect.

"Damn", she actually said out loud as she walked up slower than before, knowing full well what would greet her, other than her date. Within ten feet of being near him, he definitely committed another dating faux pois. She really contained her irritation and worked desperately to make light conversation about his job, Stacey's connection to his position at his work, and allowed him to ask a few questions. Upon finishing her cocktail and trying desperately to evade the lingering monster, she encouraged him to collect the tab and they go down to buy tickets for the go carts. "At least that way, he won't offend anyone but himself in the cart", she thought to herself, as she sent the bartender an apologetic look. Once downstairs, they cleared the green cloud, and breathing became easier. The go cart attendant said, "Sorry, but we are closing early this evening, so we can't rent you guys carts". Disappointed, her date arranged for them to play some video games, and they ordered ostrich burgers from the eatery inside. Realizing they had made it through almost an hour since the last incident, she smiled at him reassuringly and he reached over the table to hold her hand. Their conversation grew, this time engaging in much more detail about his interests and family. His intelligence intrigued her and she leaned in closer, propping her chin up on the palm of her hand, elbow on the table. He suggested suddenly, "It's getting late, I had better get you home". His quick walking was an indication of his persistent issue, and she couldn't help but wonder if the burger or cocktail had anything to do with his gassiness. Light talk continued, as she sensed an unspoken urgency on his behalf and she agreed to be taken home immediately.

Upon arriving at her apartment complex, he managed, "Well, that was fun, let me walk you to your door". Unsure if that would be a good idea, but not willing to endure the result of staying with him any longer, she replied, "That would be nice, thank you". Approaching her front door, he looked incredibly uncomfortable so she gave him a hug and said, "Goodnight", noticing the stench again and feeling sorry for her date. He looked down at his shoes, then back up at her, offering a slight smile then said, "See you at the gym". As he walked away briskly, she fumbled with her keys but her roommate opened the front door. "What the hell happened out here, it freaking smells like open ass", she exclaimed, hoping to catch them in a kiss but noticing her roommate was alone at the entry. The question insinuated that she had caused the seemingly inescapable odor, while her laughter only exacerbated the issue. "You don't want to know", the girl said, shaking her head in disappointment and pure shock of the realization that her date was a great set-up, but the evening had become a complete disaster.

The following week, he did not join the others during their lunchtime workout, and for that she was grateful. Nor did he call her again, out of pure embarrassment, or at least that was what she assumed. After a few weeks of letting the situation calm down, he came in and apologized for the terrible evening, explaining that he had eaten shellfish that day after the gym, and experienced intense food poisoning. Understanding but not willing to risk it, she told him, "We are going to be good friends", and that was that. In her opinion, if a guy isn't feeling well, and is particularly gassy, why in the world would he agree to going on a date?

11

"QUIT YOUR BELLY ACHING!" (A Man's Story)

He had been watching her for two weeks now, cocktailing at the local Americus bar in Southern Georgia. Her long, blonde hair was consistently pulled up tight in a rubber band, keeping it out of the way of drinks she was running to her patrons, and out of the path of lit cigarettes. Occasionally, she would glance his way, giving him hope and encouragement to make his advances. He envisioned her tied up locks let loose as she slowly pulled the rubber band out of her hair, shaking her hair back and forth, revealing her hidden hotness. On one drunken night, he just couldn't hold back anymore. His buddies from college were egging him on, and after a few shots, he practically tripped her to get her attention and asked, "Hey, I've been noticing you looking at me, what's your name?" Her laugh was polite but indicative of her interest as she replied in a low, sexy voice, "I think it was you who was doing all the watching. There's more where that comes from. My name is Kristy". And with that, she gave him her number with a legible ink print on the palm of his hand, to which he was certain not to lose. She walked away, shaking her ass and gave him a wink as she looked over her left shoulder. His knees seemed to go weak, as his friends were all slapping him on the ass, giving him high-fives and telling him he had to call her that night in order to get lucky. As if he didn't know that. And so he did. He called her and she invited him over to her house, offering directions as if hooking up was a regular thing for her, but he didn't care.

It was nearing midnight and her shift would soon be over. He said farewell to his friends and headed over to her house. His stomach began to rumble unexpectedly and he hoped it would soon pass, as she was going to expect his best performance that evening and he was sure to give her what she wanted. The drive from the restaurant seemed to take longer than the fifteen minutes she had promised him, and he realized this fact due largely to his profuse sweating and distracting rumbling stomach. Quickly, he pulled into a nearby 24 hour K-Mart, knowing full well there would be a restroom inside to which he could empty his bowels and be on his merry way. He parked in the first spot he saw, and he ran into the store, frantically searching for the restroom, unsure of how well he could hold back. The restroom door opened freely, and he immediately took control of a stall, giving absolutely no care as to who may be in the restroom with him. Time lapsed and he realized he had been sitting there for fifteen minutes or more, but feeling relieved. He reached over for the toilet paper but to his surprise, there was not even one square. Noticing the stall beside him had shoes, he asked for some toilet paper. Politely, a woman replied from the stall beside him, saying, "Here you go". She then laughed and flushed her toilet. Mortified, he accepted the paper, wiped as slowly as he could so she would not see his face while washing at the sink. As he heard her exit, he grabbed his pants and yanked them up, fastening his button and belt in a rush and briskly washed his hands, knowing full well he was in the Women's Restroom! He slowly opened the door, looked both ways, and ran out of K-Mart, never to return to that location again. Embarrassed, his anticipation was permanently scared away for the evening, and could not be aroused any time soon. Only a hot shower, alone, would revive his prime member into action. And with that, he drove home, alone, to shower, knowing full well a beautiful woman was being stood up whom he had watched from afar. He wondered the next day if he should call her, but decided against it, as she would only see through his weakness and somehow know the truth to why he never showed up at her doorstep, but in the Women's Restroom instead. He never saw the beautiful bar maid again.

12

"THE LICKER"
(A Woman's Story)

She had opened the new watering hole in Alpharetta called "Jimmy P's" in August, as a Cocktailer with her friend, Cheryl. Gradually, she began getting to know the other staff and eventually considered most of the staff her friends. The bartenders were a cocky bunch and one of the guys began taking an interest in her. Returning the interest, they began spending time together taking smoke breaks out the side door during evening shifts. A friendship developed but as they continued to spend time together, they knew a love interest was brewing. So not to make their working relationship awkward, she deliberately took matters slowly. During the course of a very boring Sunday afternoon shift, they got to chatting and he invited her to eat dinner the upcoming week at his home, which she accepted.

"Buckhead? You want me to meet you for dinner at your brother's house in Buckhead?" she responded, as he informed her of the whereabouts of their anticipated dinner. "Yeah, he lives in this phat house in Buckhead and he asked me to house sit. Do you mind?" Not wanting to be difficult, she agreed to meet him, despite the fact that she lived in Alpharetta, and knew he lived even further North on GA 400 than she, and wondered why he would engage in drinking and eating down in Buckhead. Instead of questioning his judgment, she just decided to risk the DUI and go with it.

As she arrived at his brother's house, the lights were dimmed, candles were lit, smooth jazz music played in the background, and he greeted her at the door with an apron wrapped around his waist. The kitchen range was lit up with steam and flame, as pots bubbled and smells emanated of cooking food. Impressed at his efforts, she gave him a kiss right on the lips, leaving a slight residue of her pink lipstick. Recalling from other dating experiences, she knew if she wanted to be kissed, not to wear crazy, rich colored lipstick. Otherwise, if she does, she will wear it all over her face by the end of the night. Luckily, she chose wisely with her tinted pink, just sheer enough to not leave evidence of an anticipated make-out session. He returned the kiss lightly, but soon began giving her directions of where to put place mats, glasses, and silverware.

The dinner comprised of steamed bass with a light lemon butter sauce, and asparagus with rice pilaf and a French loaf. He served a Clos du Bois Chardonnay with dinner, which went deliciously well with the fish. As dinner grew to a close, she began to blot her lips with a napkin. Simultaneously, he reached over to kiss her and kind of held on, as if to tell her there would be more to come. She was getting a little buzzed from the wine, and enjoyed the sudden rush of excitement she felt when he kissed her. Suggesting the couch would be more comfortable, they left the table, quickly assuming the spooning position, and snuggled as they watched a movie. There was no telling what the movie was or who starred in the film, as they were so engrossed in one another, it served as mere background noise. His manly stature extended his body six feet five inches and his legs hung clumsily off the couch. She lay on the inside dwarfed by his size and loving every minute of it. As he kissed her, she tried to keep composure and not take control. She wanted to see how he would kiss her. Slowly, he began kissing her lips, then forcing his tongue inside her mouth in a passionate, sensitive manner, turning her on to the point of no return. Sighing, she encouraged him to keep kissing her the way he was. Then, out of nowhere, he began lightly licking her lips, which at first was a major turn-on. But after a few minutes, it seemed almost creepy and dog-like, so she tried to involve her tongue but he shook his head as if to say, "let me lick you, let me do this".

Even more buzzed and dizzy from the wine and turned on than before, she let him lick her lips. But then, something awkward began to happen, as if to be a buzz kill. He began slowly licking her nose, almost inside her nostrils, and all around her mouth, then her cheeks and eventually her forehead and temples. Strangely aware of his incomplete digestion of their meal as his breath was all encompassing of her nostrils, she began to feel like this was abnormal and her interest in taking their relationship to the next level came to a screeching halt! "Wait a minute, just hold on for a second", she said with her hand trying to block the next lick as he neared her chin. Without opening his eyes, he kept moving closer to her face, as if to ignore her and continue with the licking. "Hey, wait a minute, I don't want you licking me like that, I don't care for it", she said a little louder as if to mean her statement this time. He still did not open his eyes, and began pulling her body closer to his, trying to put his tongue in her mouth. Disgusted and annoyed, she pushed him away almost yelling, "Hey, did you hear me?" Puzzled, he opened his eyes and asked, "What, you don't like to be licked"? She replied, "No, as a matter of fact the only licking I like is on a totally different body part and you're way off from that area".

Irritated at the situation, she struggled to get out from underneath his body, and walked into the kitchen to pour a glass of water. She gathered her handbag and thanked him for dinner, making a quick getaway to leave. As she drove home to Alpharetta, forty-five minutes away, she caught herself shaking her head and laughing out loud, wondering how in the world he would possibly think that she would want him to lick her in that manner. As you might imagine, working with him after that date was not easy, and she never consented to another date again, despite his requests. Imagining what he would do to her if they were to be more intimate gave her the creeps. As most employees at Jimmy P's were issued a nickname, his soon became "The Licker". Hers was given by he and he alone: "The Bitch".

13

"LOVE ON THE NET"
(A Man's Story)

He found her on MySpace and put in a friend request so they could meet. She accepted his friend request, and they began chatting on a regular basis. He thought she was totally sexy, so he invited her to a local Starbucks to meet in person. Agreeing, she walked into Starbucks that particular evening and took his breath away. Several double shots of espresso later, an hour had passed and they both decided to take his car into Midtown for a few adult beverages, offering a more rambunctious nature. The night progressed very well. The conversation flowed almost as freely as the alcohol, gently nudging him to make his move. The old, "Wanna hang out at my place and watch a movie?" usually works when there are interested parties involved. Sure enough it did. After a cloudy cab ride to his apartment, they both ended up on the couch and I'm sad to say you won't be getting an X-rated ending. Just an innocent snuggle and a quick pass out, and both were asleep like two nursing home folks after their early bird special. Oddly enough, however, at approximately four o'clock in the morning, the hot MySpace girl said she wants to go home. He suggested since they are both so drunk that she stay until later in the morning, so he can get to his car in Midtown, and drop her off up the road at hers, but she remained persistent. Reminding her of the recent shots taken together at a club, he explained that he is still very drunk, and probably shouldn't cab ride back to his car, as he would have to drive her to her car.

Determined and stubborn she states, "So I'm going to have to take a cab by myself to get to my car?" Tired of arguing, exhausted, and still drunk he responded, "I guess so". Upset and surprised of his answer, she quickly gathered her things and left his apartment. After a couple of minutes in his drunken stupor he decided that he should probably call to make sure she is all right and that she did indeed make it to her car. "Where the hell is my phone?" he said aloud, after thirty minutes of stripping his apartment. He knocked loudly on his roommate's door, asking if he could use his cell phone to call his. Still asleep but responsive, his roommate answered the door, offering his cell phone. He entered the numbers in almost a panic as he reassured himself, "It has to be here"! Not hearing his phone ringing, he assumed he must have either left his phone accidentally in the cab on the ride home from the bar, or that his hottie, MySpace girl took it. "Damnit!" he exclaimed, accepting the fact that his cell phone was officially gone. By then, it was five o'clock in the morning and he was still exhausted from the night before, so he decided not to worry about what he couldn't control, and went back to sleep on the couch.

As daylight peered through the blinds, he awoke to the realization that he had some issues to contend with that afternoon, and his mood turned sour. He reached for his pants on the coffee table to check his receipts from the previous evening, and realized his wallet was missing. Panic set in and he yelled, "Where in the hell is my wallet?" By now, his roommate was awake and in the kitchen, shaking his head as if to know his friend had these sorts of debacles, while he opened the refrigerator door and grabbed the orange juice. "Dude, really, when are you going to get off MySpace?"

Oddly enough after an hour of searching the apartment, his roommate informed him that someone called his phone saying they found a phone on the street right outside of the Starbucks that he had met the girl. Also, his roommate claimed he tried calling his cell phone a few times while he was asleep, someone answered but quickly hung up, sending the call to his voice mail. They both figured that the MySpace girl hurled his phone out of a moving vehicle, and hit the ground near the infamous Starbucks. His wallet was assumed to be their love memento, as he never saw the girl again. Sadly, he continued claiming the single status of "Man Seeking Woman" online.

14

"INDIGESTION MAN"
(A Woman's Story)

A young woman was hanging out with some collegiate friends at a Harvard Law campus bar one Fall night when she met him. Initially, his tipsy approach seemed irritating, but his devilish charm and whit grew on her. After talking for a while, he asked her for her phone number, which she reluctantly issued due to his inebriation. Luckily, he remained coherent enough to remember to actually use it. The very next day, she received a phone call from him with a casual dinner invitation, which she graciously accepted. Before the phone conversation ended, he also offered to pick her up since the Dolphin Seafood Restaurant was only a few miles away from her place on Massachusetts Avenue. Greeting her at her front door with his debonair smile, he wore the classic law student garb: a crisp, long-sleeved, striped oxford shirt with khaki shorts. Anticipating his attire, she chose a simple sun dress with a light sweater, a feeble attempt at looking sexy despite their casual dinner. Although she had never been to this restaurant before, the hearsay was that it bore a fine meal, so she grew excited for what the evening had to offer with her new beau.

She seemed to be taking in his every move as he exuded chivalry with both his greeting at the front door and as he opened her car door, which impressed a smile on her face. His demeanor was calm and reserved, as he was a contented man. "After all, he drove a brand new Porsche!" she thought to herself as they drove out of her driveway. They neared the Dolphin and he asked her to stay in the car so he could open her car door for her. "What a gentleman", she thought to herself. Accustomed to providing for herself, the attention was refreshing and a nice change to the usual idiots she had been dating.

As they were greeted by the hostess and sat for their dinner reservation, he proceeded to order a Miller Lite then asked her if she would care for a beer. Reluctant, as she never drinks beer, she ordered a Michelob Ultra Amber knowing she would really regret that move later. Beer made her burp and she knew it could lead to a disaster, but felt she should adapt to this casual seafood environment and enjoy herself. The appetizers of calamari and seafood gumbo were ordered and consumed along with a few more beers for each of them. The main courses arrived and by then, they had been kissing and eating and laughing and making a mess with crab, shrimp, clams and lobster shells. Just as she was thinking to herself, "This has been a fun date", he reached over to her without warning and kissed her with an open mouth, except instead of a kiss, she received a burp followed by vomit. It wasn't that he fully puked into her mouth, but it was that acid reflux type of burp with an accidental vomit residue left over that trickled into her mouth, resulting with a face of disgust. She was sure he realized what had happened because he looked mortified as she was unsure of what to say or do, other than repeatedly wash out her mouth with the remaining water on the table. She knew if she did not wash out her mouth, she would puke for sure. Needless to say, their date became irreparable and he politely drove her home. They did not go out again. She often wondered if she should have given him another chance, since accidents do happen, but she just couldn't take the risk or thought of kissing him again. Lesson to be learned is despite your high class charm, never offer your date a slurpy, burpy kiss during dinner, as they may find your bile to be vile.

15

"Smoking Hot Psycho"
(A Man's Story)

Two guys went out one night to a hip martini bar in Atlanta, when one of them ran into an old flame. She had some friends with her and the introductions were made. Just as they walked away, the other guy said, "Dude, your old girl's friend is hot, what's her story". The guy said, "Yeah, she's hot, but she's one crazy bitch". Not really surprised by his friend's claim, as many girls he had met recently bore that title, he replied frankly, "Yeah, but I still think she's smoking hot! I'm going to talk to her, see what she's all about. I will catch up with you later on". His friend just shook his head and they parted ways. After approaching her group at a cocktail table, he reintroduced himself and they began chatting, eventually asking her for her digits then he left to find his friend.

A few days later, the standard waiting period for making the first call to a girl, he made his move and asked her out for a dinner date, despite being forewarned that the girl he was interested in was a nut case. He was certain of proving his friend wrong about this girl. He chose the Lobster Bar at Chops in Buckhead, as he felt it was hip and swank enough to impress her.

They ate a nice meal, drank some fine red wine, and at the end of dinner he began to think to himself, "She's not nutty, she's hot!" Just as he completed the thought, she begins to pick her teeth with her pinky nail, which is totally turning him off! His wine buzz had kicked in and he was feeling full and content, but irritated at his date's gesture. Suggesting they head over to Twisted Taco as he paid the check, she agreed and excused herself to go to the ladies room. In the lobby, he ran into his friend who told him about his nutty date, who also was on a date at the Lobster Bar. Comments were exchanged about their evening and his friend's date walked up, asking if he would take a picture of them. The guy obliged and took a few pictures. After a few minutes of picture taking, his date came out of the bathroom and totally wigged out on him, accusing him of hitting on the girl that was with his friend. Shocked and embarrassed at the false accusation, he tried to explain to the "nut case" that he was simply taking pictures at his friend's request and that she need not worry. After all the confusion, the guy still thinks his crazy date is too hot to take home for the evening and accepts her offer to go back to her place for a drink. She says she doesn't want to sleep with him, due to the fact that it's their first date together, but she wants to change into something more comfortable, so she went into her bedroom, and returned with a bustier and pajama bottoms.

Wondering how in the hell he would be able to control himself with her rocking body properly revealed in the bustier, he chose to sit at the opposite end of the couch, and just faced her asking, "So, where is this drink I have heard so much about?". Her siren expression changed to an irritated one and she said, "It's over there in the liquor cabinet, go get it yourself!" A little worried that the warning generously offered by his friend earlier in the week may be revealed at this very moment, he jumped off the couch and opened the cabinet. There was a variety of liquors but nothing he found appetizing. He thought if making a joke, that it may lighten the heavy air in the room so he braved, "Do you want a Banana Split or Chocolate Martini, because I know how to make both." She whipped her long hair around and caught him in the eye with a few strands, stinging his eye and making him teary. He dropped the banana liquor bottle he was holding, shattering the yellow, sticky fluid on her carpet, which created a disgusting, banana mess. "You idiot!" she yelled with a red, crazy-eyed face, which scared him out of wanting a drink. She stomped out of the room and grabbed some towels from the hallway closet, then plopped down on the floor and fumed, "I hope you don't think you are getting any action out of me tonight, I mean, you will just have to wait until our next date. This really pisses me off!" Shocked at the intensity of the moment and how quickly they arrived at such a moment, he apologized for the spill and offered to pay for the carpet cleaning. She refused his offer and told him to leave, which he did promptly without regret.

Once he arrived safely inside his car and he turned the engine on, he called his forewarning friend to report the disastrous evening, and for a good laugh. He swore that he would never ignore a friend's warning again, that it was too powerful of a dating tool, and that he would never speak to the girl again. Too bad, he thought, because that bustier would have looked better on her floor.

16

"The Wrestler"
(A Woman's Story)

A recently divorced girl had a profile on My Space, who received a message by a local hair stylist. Hesitant to message him back, she waited a day before responding. After a few more messages from him, she caved and responded to his questions. Persistent, he continued to send messages to her, eventually asking her if they could meet in person at a nearby Starbucks. Nervous, but needing to get out and back into the dating scene again, she agreed to meet him and answered him back with a flirtatious reply. His charm and whit were enough for her to decide to meet him.

She arrived before he did, and found a window seat, hoping to catch a glimpse of him before he noticed her. Just as she looked away for a moment, he walked in, looking a little different than his My Space picture. He walked over to her and formerly introduced himself, smiling as if he were surprised that she looked exactly like her photos. He suggested they get a coffee, and as they approached the counter, he orders his coffee first and then looks at her as if it were naturally her turn next. The cashier picked up on the awkwardness, and deliberately looked to him to collect for the order. He started feeling his front pockets and back pant pockets only to exclaim, "Oh damn, I forgot my wallet! I'm really sorry, I will make it up to you, ok". Ordinarily, she wouldn't mind buying someone a drink but typically not on a first date, and certainly not after he had made the suggestion. Either way, someone had to pay for the coffees, so the girl reluctantly offered up her debit card. His cavalier attitude was beginning to irritate her as he thanked her, and began walking over towards some unoccupied chairs in a corner as if she should follow him. During their conversation, which mainly consisted of himself, the guy mentioned that his Toyota Celica outside had an amazing sound system and he wanted her to hear one of his favorite songs.

It was a very hot May afternoon, and as she entered his car, it was noticeably hot and stuffy as his air conditioner did not work properly. There was also a very strange stench emitting from his vents that resembled a cheap cigar. "What is that smell?" she asked without hesitation and out of pure disgust. "Oh, that, well, I smoked some Swisher Sweets in here the past few days and it must be that". After about an hour of inhaling stale cigar fumes and suffering from near heat stroke, the bass from his system was becoming overwhelming and she asked to excuse herself. Picking up on her need to get some water and cool off, he asked if they could go somewhere else to talk. She suggested her place in Alpharetta, but that it was thirty minutes away. He said he didn't mind the drive, and asked if they could get something to eat because he was really hungry. Another red flag that she obviously missed, she suggested he follow behind her in his car and they could stop somewhere along the way to eat.

After eating at a sandwich shop in Alpharetta, he followed her to her house and immediately she needed a cocktail to relax, suggesting, "Do you want to take a shower". Assuming she was insinuating that her suggestion of a shower meant sex, he walked up to her and began kissing her passionately. Grossed out due to the lingering fumes of the stale cigars, she reiterated, "No, seriously, you need to get that smell off of you before I can kiss you again, it's really bad, and now I really need a drink. Do you want one?" He obliged and, as she was pouring the juice into the glass, he laid down on the carpet in the living room and stated abruptly, "Do you want to wrestle?" Now she's really confused. "No", she stated, almost questioning his intentions and the nature of this wrestle match. "Why not? I told you I am a Brazilian Ju Jitzu wrestler. Come on, let's spar!" Not realizing what she was getting herself into, she agreed but only if she could finish her drink first. He watched her intently as she sipped the last bit of liquid from her glass, then quickly grabbing her by her waist and pulling her onto the floor, putting her into a very sexual position. He began squeezing his legs around her, which was very uncomfortable and was beginning to hurt, forcing her to find a way to get out of this wrestling hold. Not amused but trying desperately to break free, she was not a strong enough opponent, and his laughter began to inflame her. Frustrated but trying to keep her composure, she did not want to upset him as he was a perfect stranger in her house who was trying to see if she can get away from him. Scary. After several attempts without success, she failed at getting away from him or out of his holds. As his laughter continued, she began to speak in a firmer tone, which encouraged him to whip his leg around, pinning her in the most awkward position and simultaneously hitting the side of her head in the process. She screamed in her mind, "I'm going to be bruised from this idiot, I just know it!" It was this frustration and infuriation that allowed her to finally break free from his firm grip. Trying to resist kicking him in the nuts for putting her through that torture, she stated loudly, "What in the hell do you think you are doing here? I do not appreciate you being so rough with me, and I do not want to wrestle anymore. I think you should leave!" He left without saying "Thank you for dealing with my weird ass", and even tried to keep in touch with her by sending more messages on My Space. Shortly thereafter, she was informed of how to set her profile to private, responding to his last message, "Go wrestle yourself!"

17

"THE QUICKIE"
(A Man's Story)

He was the third wheel on a boating trip with some friends in Key West, when he spotted her on her family's yacht. He was scrubbing down the front of his friend's boat and drinking a beer as her boat floated past, and she was hot and totally eye-balling him. At some point, they had met once both boats were docked, and they decided to go to a nearby restaurant and have a drink. Within thirty minutes of being in the bar area, they began to kiss and she suggested they go to the bathroom to make-out. He obliged and followed her into the women's bathroom, locking the door behind him. They were going at it, and having sex so passionately, that they hardly noticed the noise they produced from inside the tiled bathroom. As they were finished and laughing at their hurried sexual encounter, they exited the bathroom, only to receive a standing ovation from the table of eight sitting just outside the bathroom.

Mortified, the girl walked briskly by the table while covering her face with her hand. He was appreciative of the clapping, and actually said "Thank you" as he bowed and laughed. He also left the restaurant, and met up with his friends on their boat. Later on that afternoon, he saw the girl again, only to be ignored as she felt humiliated at her behavior, and the table's obnoxious response. They never saw each other again, but he loved being able to say he had hot love on the docks.

18

"HIGH EXPECTATIONS"
(A Woman's Story)

She met a guy who attended M.I.T., who also happened to grow marijuana in Western Massachusetts. He invited her out one night to dinner and she accepted, not realizing what she was getting herself into that evening.

He picked her up in his five year old BMW, top down, with a lit cigarette in his mouth, and honked the horn twice as he entered her driveway. Disgusted at her date's horn honking, she peeled back the window curtain and shook her head. She had a bad feeling about this guy at this point but decided to go through with the date anyway, since she didn't have anything else better to do that Tuesday evening. She walked outside towards his car and he exited his car, just in time to throw his cigarette out onto her lawn. He greeted her with a kiss on her cheek then in a chivalrous move, he opened her car door. In a weird sort of way, he acted very comfortable with her despite the fact that she hardly knew him. Curious to see how this date would turn out, she smiled back at him, completing the initial greeting.

They drove to a local steakhouse and ate mediocre meals, as she thought he would have suggested a steakhouse with some sort of flare. She was mostly unimpressed at his inability to select a complimentary wine to accompany the meal, and the twenty dollar bottle went down in a harsh way. "Here we go", she thought as he gulped down his food and wine, all the while trying to engage her in some sort of random and deep conversation about how his studies were all encompassing of how the world went around. Her thoughts were of her cozy couch at the house and how she wanted to be sitting on it, away from this numb skull. Before she knew it, he ordered another bottle of the same crappy wine, yet her glass remained full. Politely, she continued to take the occasional sip here and there while he gabbed on and on about himself. As he put a major dent in the second bottle of wine, his conversation began to die down and he asked if she wanted to go back to his place to smoke out. Thinking back at the last time she had actually smoked weed, she agreed, thinking it could change the course of events for the evening, despite his lack of charm. He paid the check and they left the steakhouse, eventually arriving at his humble one acre, three-story home on the hill in a very posh neighborhood. His home was the only one, however, that seemed to boast a dream catcher in the kitchen window. She realized this guy was a hippie at M.I.T., and would always be a hippie, despite his future endeavors.

His home was cozy and his couch became very inviting. Giving her the quick tour of his home, he excused himself for a minute as he went into the study to unlock his drawer, and retrieve some of the greenest, stinkiest weed she had ever experienced! His face lit up with pride as he presented the bag to her, and then he escorted her into his living room in the basement. It was a perfect set up for hanging out in the illegal sense, and so she immediately felt at ease. As they passed around a joint, and the high began to kick in, she noticed his conversation was getting deep again, and she wanted him to shut up so she laid a huge kiss on him. He shut up for a minute or two, which was nice since his kiss was wet and sloppy, but when you are both silly and high, the kiss seems really good. As soon as she pulled away, he requested, "Would you please masturbate with that tomato over there? I would love it if you would masturbate with that tomato". Shocked and very high, she lazily glanced in the direction in which he was pointing towards a tomato on a table. "Random", she said out loud, and unsure if she should take his request seriously, but he kept asking her to perform this obnoxious act. She declined with a very definite, "No", but his persistence became intensified. He had asked her about six times now, not letting up, which was really irritating her. With a huff, she got off the couch, walked over to the tomato, picked it up, and squished it in her hand, then threw it at him, allowing it to splatter all over him and his couch. She laughed out loud, which only pissed him off. She laughed even louder, pointing at the tomato goo that was hanging off his chin. He was really upset now, and demanded that she go home. As she continued to laugh, she reminded him that he had picked her up and that he had to take her home, which was perfectly fine by her at that point. High or not, she totally did not mind his driving, as he was finally silent for the first time the entire evening. The top to his BMW was down complementing the gorgeous, evening weather. She closed her eyes, tried to enjoy her high and the wind blowing through her hair as they sat in silence. Knowing his strange ways would never change, she graciously thanked him for dinner, and exited his car as he sped out of her driveway. His lack of grace allowed her to forget all about him and she never saw him again. Maybe she never heard from him because he found someone to fulfill his high expectations?

19

"DUDE LOOKED LIKE A LADY" (A Man's Story)

Two guys driving through a college town grew weary of their travels so they checked into the glamorous Motel 6 for the evening. After showering, separately of course, they felt energized enough to go out and hit the local bars, which were just a quarter mile walk away from their accommodations. Assuming they would each be hooking up with hot chicks later, they put their dirty clothes away in their suitcases, and tidied up the hotel room before leaving.

Once on the strip, they strutted like pathetic peacocks, hoping to find either a good buzz or an unsuspecting lover. Luckily, two girls approached them, both smiling and eager to meet them. What luck! And they are both hot too! Without hesitation, the girls were invited to do numerous shots at the nearest bar, and then to go back to their hotel room, upon which they happily obliged. The Motel 6 glistened in the night and the closer they got to the hotel, the more the girls gathered and began whispering. This only made the guys nervous, each asking the other, "Dude, which one do you like?" After making their decisions, they immediately walked over and began putting on the moves hard to their woman of choice.

The hotel room door swung open to reveal the two double beds, and almost simultaneously, each guy picked up his chosen bitch and began kissing her passionately. The girls confirmed their moves leaving no room for hesitation. Through his drunken haze, one of the guys looked over witnessing his buddy going at it with his girl of choice, which at first didn't seem so awkward. Blushing, he looked down at his lady and suddenly realized that she had an Adam's Apple. It was a man!! "What the hell, dude, it's a dude!" the guy practically screamed, pushing the He-She off his bed. His friend looked up for a moment, not sure what was happening, and went back to what he was doing, which was the new girl in his bed. Abruptly, the door flung open and the guy escorted the He-She out of the room, then he threw His-Her clothes out of the window in mortified disgust. Moments later, the guy's friend finished up and excused himself to use the bathroom, motioning for his obviously upset friend to join him to discuss the unfortunate events. He exclaimed, "She was a He!" Desperately trying to contain his laughter, but also embarrassed for his friend, the guy asked if he could at least continue his hook up and the disturbed guy left the hotel room, knowing full well he would catch holy hell the next morning on their ride home. The "He-She" was never seen or heard from again, as the unmatched couple failed to exchange phone numbers in the beginning of the evening. Even if they did, who would be the "guy" to make the first call?

20

"THE MISSING MEMBER"
(A Woman's Story)

Two old high school girlfriends moved in together while attending college. The twosome thoroughly enjoyed visiting their limited local bar scene. One night after extensive primping and irrational thinking about what to wear, they were picked up by another girlfriend and hit the bars. Her roommate's boyfriend, Stuart, greeted them at Paradise, a bar where he was employed, and passed out a round of tequila shots. The other roommate turned around and noticed that the cutest guy she had ever seen was staring at her. His smile was genuine and he walked over to say "hello". Everything about this guy was perfect, even down to the hairs on his head. After lengthy discussion, her roommate came over and introduced herself along with their other friend, inviting the new guy back to their place to hangout as the bar was about to close. He obliged and rode along with the girls, with their promise to give him a ride home whenever he was ready to leave.

The new guy's chivalry of opening her car door, buying her drinks, and polite conversation had impressed her, as she began leaning into his words, trying to hint of a desired kiss before the end of the evening. He caught onto this move, of course, and planted a big one on her while in the cramped car, creating an awkward silence amongst the ladies. The radio was turned up, due to the uncomfortable slurping sounds, and they pulled into the driveway of their apartment complex. "Okay, we're here", as if to announce to the couple making out in the back seat, "Hey, you can take a breather for a moment!" Giggling, the couple pulled away, but still clung onto one another as if one might be lost in the unloading of the car. Just shortly inside the apartment, Stuart phoned to report he would not be dropping by, and within that moment, the couple dashed into her bedroom to have some privacy. "Great, that's just great. Stuart isn't coming over and they are in there, so I guess it's just you and me", the roommate said to her girlfriend who picked them up earlier in the evening. The girlfriend responded quickly, "No it's not, I'm heading home! I gotta get up early tomorrow". Disappointed but understanding, the roommate hugged her girlfriend and said farewell, letting the door slam shut on it's own as if to say, "Are you two happy? Everyone has left so have fun in there!" The roommate went straight to her bedroom, not to be notified through the walls as to the activity behind closed doors.

The next morning, the roommates met in the living room, and through whispers they discussed the specifics of the previous evening, and more specifically, of her roommate's hook-up. The roommate looked like she had seen a ghost! "What happened last night? Is everything alright?" the one girl asked her roommate. "Go look in the freezer", she responded almost in disbelief, cupping her face in her hands. Unsure of what she would find, and giving her roommate an uneasy glance, the roommate opened the freezer and gasped, "What the hell is that?!" Giggling and grimacing, she slowly pulled from the icy cave a prosthetic leg, one that began above the knee extending to a stiff foot. They shook their heads in disbelief, both wondering how it had fit inside so perfectly and laughing low. "Shhhhhh!!" her roommate laughed and hand-motioned, to keep the responses to a minimum, as her new beau was still in her bed, contently sleeping off last evening's charades. Apparently, as they were making out he removed his prosthetic leg, thinking it would somehow break the ice of his missing appendage. He even went so far as to put it in the freezer for her roommate to find in the morning. Much to his surprise, his hook-up was not amused and appalled actually at his insensitivity, which led the girl to deny his future advances of another date. However, if he had removed his member while driving, that would have sealed the deal!

21

"ELEMENT OF SURPRISE"
(A Man's Story)

A High School Senior had been dating the same High School Junior for the past four years, and he didn't think things were going as well as they used to, so he asked a Sophomore girl to go out with him. The Sophomore hesitantly accepted his invitation, as she was well aware of his relationship with his girlfriend. After all, they did attend the same school.

The Sophomore girl agreed to drive to his house so she could meet his parents. Much to his surprise, his Junior girlfriend had a key to his house, as his family fully trusted her, giving her permission to come over after school. She also would feed their dog, Rusty, whenever his family traveled out of town for the holidays. With that said, the Junior girlfriend drove over to his house to literally surprise him, hoping to create a "Date Night" with him, as she also sensed their relationship was on the rocks. As he saw her pull into the driveway, he panicked and tried to think of some way to get the other woman out of his house. He turned around as if to shove his new girl in a closet but his younger sister, a Freshman at the same school, entered the house through the back door, noticing the new girl in her living room. "Hey, aren't you a Sophomore at our school", his younger sister asked as she gave her brother an accusing glare. "Uh, yeah, I am, and you must be his younger sister, Jessica, a Freshman, right?" Just then, the front door opened, and his Junior girlfriend stood in the foyer with the key in her hand, walking right in and saying, "Baby, where are you?" She giggled for a moment, wondering what he must be doing, and then she noticed them on the couch, accusing "Oh my god! Who are you and what are you doing with my boyfriend?" They were just sitting on the couch, but it was the look on everyone's faces that gave them all away. The Junior girlfriend proceeded to approach her boyfriend with accusations, pointing fingers and occasional girlie punches to his left arm, as she is right handed.

"Hey, quit hitting me", he screamed in terror. She went ballistic on him and screamed right back, effectively reminding him of their relationship now lacking love, trust, and faithfulness. "I can't believe you would cheat on me, you BASTARD!" she cried. Jessica, who was frozen stiff for about ten minutes out of disbelief, finally pulled herself together and coaxed the Junior girl into her bedroom, to allow the Sophomore girl to leave without any physical altercation. Eventually, the boyfriend's Mom came on the scene, having to calm the Junior girl down, and then drove her home, as she was too upset to drive. The Junior girlfriend's car was left at the boy's house, further deterring the new Sophomore girl from dropping by. Just goes to show you, never underestimate the element of surprise!

22

"Catch & Release"
(A Woman's Story)

She had way too many Jack & Cokes one night while partying with friends in an Auburn University college bar. After downing a shot sent over by the bartender, she was brazenly approached by a hot young man sporting multiple Mardi Gras beads around his neck. He barely said a word in greeting before she fell into his lips, and began kissing him. Eventually, they left the bar together as the Kissing Bandit struck again!

The next thing she remembered is that he has taken her to his house where they were making out passionately, and also continued to drink heavily. She does not recall how she was handcuffed, as she realized her hands were bound above her head. She began to look around the room in her drunken haze and tried to focus on the guy going into his closet, noticing he opened a fireproof lock box. Inside this mystery box was a very large, blue dildo and some Crisco shortening, which he proudly displayed upon his return to the bed. A very strange feeling overwhelmed her, as she was suddenly realizing that he was intending on using this enormous dildo on her, not to mention the issues that would come if he used the Crisco as well! "Oh shit", she exclaimed. Then in more of a whimper, she begged, "Please release me". Her words were slurred and slushy, but she repeated herself over and over again to be sure she was heard. His worthless convincing, "This will be fun, you will love it, I promise", didn't seem to work as she wiggled and squirmed, continuing to state the same request. He continued to approach her but she confirmed her request in a firmer tone, "Release me now, psycho!" which seemed to convince him of reality.

Reluctantly, he agreed to unlock the handcuffs, and put back the dildo and Crisco in his fireproof lock box. Relieved and sober, she realized that her car was still at the bar where they had met. She thought that he was the last person she would want to ride with again but felt he was the only person available, so she asked him to take her back to the bar, which he drunkenly obliged. Completely disgusted with herself for allowing this ridiculous situation to become this blown out of proportion, she exited his car with a slam, hoping to never bump into him again at a local bar. And truly relieved that she had been released from his captivity!

23

"Cheap Date"
(A Man's Story)

A guy met a girl on Match dot com, who seemed normal and possessed admirable personality traits, so after talking on the phone a few times, he asked her out for drinks. He suggested the bar at a restaurant, Capital Grille, which is situated in the heart of Buckhead, a prominent area of Atlanta. As he arrived early, he quickly scoped the ladies already sitting at the bar, wondering if any of them would be his mystery date. His phone buzzed that a text had been received, stating she was running late, so he bellied up to the bar, found an extra stool for her, and ordered himself a Makers Mark and soda. Sipping slowly, he managed to finish his cocktail thirty minutes after the original meeting time, and he was beginning to feel a bit stood up. Just as he was about to give up, she walked in the front door and took his breath away. Relieved, she was just as beautiful as her picture on Match, which isn't always the case with online dating. After greeting him with a kiss on his cheek, she complimented him on his choice of restaurant, and gracefully sat down on the stool beside him.

After some small talk, he asked what she would like to drink. She assumed, "Well, I hear this is a very nice place to eat! Why don't we just order a bottle of wine and ask for a table for dinner?" Stunned at her brazen response, he said, "Why not?" Her innocence and sweet smile convinced him that dining at the restaurant was a good idea, so he ordered her a glass of wine as a starter, gave the bartender his Visa to hold open the tab, and casually walked over to the hostess stand to reserve a table. Being that it was a Friday night, the wait time at 7pm would be an hour so he prepared himself to become a little tipsy at the bar. Three drinks later, their table was available, as he was notified by the hostess tapping him on the shoulder. After closing the tab at the bar, the couple was escorted to their table for two.

As the hostess gave them each menus, she then moved to place the wine list in the middle of the table. Intercepting the move, his date grabbed the wine list and said confidently, "I will take that", as she reached over with a reassuring smile. Briefly searching the list, she requested of the hostess, "We will have a bottle of this one, I've been drinking it at the bar already". He just looks at his date like she had control of the situation, not realizing how much money the bottle of wine would cost. As they began ordering dinner, the server mentioned the Surf and Turf special, which she immediately ordered, so he just ordered a filet mignon and a side item, also not realizing how much the dishes would cost. After dinner, the server suggested dessert upon which his date gladly orders for them both, and neither of which he wants. It was about half way through dinner that he began wondering just how he had lost control during this encounter.

Once drinks, dinner, and dessert were finished, the server proudly presented the check to him, and walked away. He coyly glanced at the total and began calculating the tip to be figured in as his date went on and on about her day and her boring job. He relentlessly forfeited his Visa again to pay for dinner, knowing full well it had been well over the fifty dollars he had originally planned on spending on their first date. He also realized that the evening was not quite over, as his date began offering options of where to have after dinner drinks next. His first thought was, "I want to go home." Suppressing his thoughts, he suggested Brio, which was a typical Wednesday night hang out and home of the Wednesday Night Drinking Club in Atlanta. So they headed to Brio, and drove separately, which she conveniently parked her own car rather than the valet.

Upon meeting in the front lobby, she ordered, "I'll have a cosmopolitan", as she disappeared into the ladies room. Irritated, he ordered her drink from the bartender, ordering water for himself. Suddenly, his most recent ex-girlfriend walked up to him while he picked up his drinks, and they exchanged greetings. Minutes later, his date walked up behind his ex-girlfriend and looked upset. Not wanting his date to feel insecure about the other woman, he encouraged her to stand next to him, made the introductions, and placed his hand around her waist. The contention between the two women intensified, as his date just stared at his ex-girlfriend as if to say, "He's mine, bitch, so just walk away now!" It was at this instant that he noticed his date had a price tag hanging from the back of her shirt. Believing it would be a nice gesture, he pulled off the tag, taking extra care to not damage the fabric. Noticing the sale sticker on the price tag, he smiled thinking it was the right thing to do. Realizing what he had done, his date spun around in disgust, stating, "I wish you had not done that, I was planning on returning this shirt". Embarrassed for both of them, his ex-girlfriend said farewell to the guy and left the scene. The guy was totally mortified of this dating experience so he left his date's side with a brief farewell, went to the bar to pay his tab one last time, and headed toward valet to obtain his car. He never contacted or saw the disturbed woman again, and eventually got off Match dot com all together, regretting his option of online dating.

24

"ANOTHER MATCH, MADE IN HELL"
(A Woman's Story)

A middle-aged woman was convinced that paying to be on Match dot com would be a wise investment, so she agreed to meet one of her "matches" out one night. They had been chatting online and on the phone for about two weeks before meeting face-to-face, so the anticipation of meeting was high. It was a hot summer night, as a busy Friday drinking crowd gathered at the local cantina Rio Grande. He had chosen the hot spot, agreeing to grab a table outside, since the beautiful and breezy weather practically screamed for patio dining. He called her as she was rounding the corner of the restaurant, and she confirmed her entrance. As she walked out onto the patio, searching the crowd through her designer sunglasses, she spotted him. His handsome and stylish posture was just as she remembered on the Match dot com site, bringing a feverish smile to her face.

They anxiously greeted one another with a hug both saying, "Hey, so nice to finally meet you" and "Hey, you look great". Just as she was about to take a seat, she heard her name being called by a familiar voice from another table. Turning around, she realized it was one of her best friends and her boyfriend sitting just one row away from their table. She smiled and said, "Hey Kimmie, Hey Chris!", and approached their table. The two women hugged as she made the introductions to her date. The other men at their table were unknown to her so she allowed Kimmie to make the introductions for everyone else. Seemingly perplexed at the coincidence of the two women being at the same location on the same evening, he said, "It's nice to meet you" and then looked away as if he didn't want to talk anymore. The awkward moment caused Kimmie to say, "You two have fun, and I'll call you later tonight, okay". Picking up on her friend's hint, she sat down at the table with her date, catching his uncomfortable glare. Unsure of how to read him, she suggested that they join the table with her friends, thinking that may break the tension that was so thick between them. He said that would be fine but needed to step outside to make a phone call first. "I will be right back", he reassured her, as he walked back into the restaurant searching through his cellular phone.

Kimmie encouraged her to join them at their table, as she was curious about the details of her date, her membership on Match dot com, and about how excited she was to finally meet him. Happening to look toward the front door of the restaurant, she noticed her date was leaving, walking briskly toward the valet to retrieve his car. "What the hell is he doing?" she exclaimed as she fumbled around in her handbag for her cellular phone to catch him before he left. Snickering that he left, Kimmie said, "I guess he wanted to be alone with you". Humiliated, she hung her head out of embarrassment. "How could he just up and leave like that, I mean, who does that?" she wined in disbelief as tears welled up in her eyes. He finally answered her phone call after several attempts explaining, "Yeah, you planned this all along! You knew your friends would be here to judge me and I didn't appreciate it!" Her jaw was still hanging to the floor, but she managed to defend, "You were the one who suggested the location to meet me tonight and I had no idea they would be here, honest!" His silence was evident that she was right and his leaving was a blessing in disguise. Kimmie gave her friend a good hug and said, "Let me buy you a margarita, girlie, and forget about that stupid guy from Match". She decided to stick around with her friends, consuming large quantities of top shelf margaritas. Upon entering her home later that evening, she promptly canceled her Match dot com membership, to minimize the risk of meeting any more lame men.

25

"KNEE POPPER"
(A Man's Story)

A guy is introduced to a girl from a mutual friend, and eventually asks her out to dinner. After a fine meal, they head to her house and begin sealing the deal. His actions are more animated than she expected, as she tried desperately to keep her form and participation in tact, while he manhandled her for at least an hour. Suddenly, he flipped her over and began thrusting as hard as he could when he heard a blood-curdling scream, "Oh my gosh, my knee!" Her face turned white as she announced the dislocation of her knee. He looked down and nearly hurled as he realized what had happened. Her left knee had popped out of socked, and was cocked even more to the left and she lay paralyzed by pain. "Holy Shit! What do I do, I mean, do I call the ambulance or what?" he said in a panicked tone as he quickly scanned the house for a telephone. He called the ambulance as soon as he spotted the phone in the kitchen, and the paramedics quickly arrived on the scene. All the while he tried to calm her down, confirming he was still interested in her, but that this had him freaked out a bit. She understood and proceeded to explain to him that this had happened before, but not on another date, and that it would be ok. He helped her get a sundress and underwear on so she would be covered before the ambulance arrived, and she was very grateful but incredibly embarrassed.

The next day, he called up the best florist in town, ordering the biggest bouquet of flowers to be delivered to her home. She had to have her knee reset and a full leg cast set, and had taken the next day off. As the week progressed, the two exchanged phone calls of how their lovemaking session had been so rudely interrupted by the unfortunate event of her knee popping out, and proceeded to plan a second run on the matter. The night of gratuitous lovemaking would commence the upcoming Friday evening, after he prepared dinner in her home and assumed consumption of a bottle of merlot. Good sex WAS possible with a woman with a full leg cast, although the unfortunate event never really left his mind.

26

"BEER GOGGLES"
(A Woman's Story)

A very buxom, middle-aged woman drove her fabulous Jaguar to the local Mellow Mushroom to hangout with her gays when he approached the table as their server saying, "Hey, my name is Nick, what can I get you to drink?" He was about five foot seven with dark brown hair and hazel eyes, staring down her cleavage like he wanted to take her home that very minute. His dancing eyes moved all over her body, and she was hooked line and sinker! Three pitchers of beer and two hours later, he had been sealing the deal, hoping to become invited to her house after his shift. She lived nearby in the cutest little home, and he had been hearing her boisterous voice carry across the restaurant, enticing him even more to get to know her, so he decided to invite himself. She did not object, in fact, she became filled with anticipation as it had been a whole week since a man had held her in his arms.

As the discounted check was laid before them, he scribbled his cellular number along the top, adding, "I would very much like to see you tonight after work, would that be okay with you?" Blushing, she responded, "What time do you get off?" They discussed the juicy details and time he wanted her to come back to pick him up, and she left with her friends, all giggling and drunk with laughter.

She hurried home, took a long, sudsy shower and dreamed of how the evening would proceed once he came back to her place. She hoped he would sweep her off her feet with a decent make-out session, but didn't want to get her hopes up so she got dressed to pick him up and hoped for the best. Arriving on time, he jumped into her Jaguar saying too loudly, "Damn, girl, I hit the jackpot!" Stunned at the accent he used and the way he plopped down into the passenger seat, almost pulling off a Dukes of Hazard maneuver, she replied, "Thanks, I guess." It was a little awkward at first, but they soon got over it, and resumed the flirting that initialized in the restaurant. "So, what do you want to do with me?", she asked. Confident in his ability to satisfy her, he said while putting his left arm over the headrest of her seat, "You just wait, it's gonna be great!" "Huh", she thought to herself, as she had been charmed by more enchanting fellows. As they pulled into her driveway, he anxiously jumped out of her car to open her car door for her, practically yanking her out of her side. "Whoa, whoa, whoa", she said trying to calm him down, as if he hadn't been with a woman in an even longer time. "Sorry, I just really like you, I can't help it", and with that they entered her home for what she calls the longest one-night-stand she had ever had.

Three days later, she emerged exhausted and felt like a bad friend for not contacting her girlfriend, informing her of the details of her date. As the story unfolded, she exclaimed, "He was such an amazing lover, seriously, I mean, he could do things with his tongue that I have never imagined until now!" Her girlfriend listened intently to every word as they laughed about the reason he had left. "You wouldn't believe it, I mean, I was kissing him and it was like the third day of him being at my place, sex all day, eating when we were hungry, partying like rock stars, and I suddenly realized something. He had nubs for teeth!" "No way", her friend shrieked in disbelief, "Really? No teeth? I can't believe you never noticed!" She had to take a minute to stop as she felt like vomiting while recalling the story. "Yeah, it was so weird because he when talked to me, I guess I just never noticed his missing teeth." Evidently, he would talk with his lips covering his gum line, never exposing his missing munchers, and he has dentures but never wears them. The woman continued, "And get this, he confided in me that he lost his teeth because he used to smoke a lot of crack and snort a lot of crystal meth, and it was cheaper for him to get his teeth pulled rather than do the work to save them!" "Nice", her friend responded shaking her head in disappointment, recognizing that on a sober level her friend would have made a wiser choice in men. Turned out, the toothless wonder, who worked at a pizza joint, had a seven-month pregnant girlfriend he was living with at the Extended Stay when all this went down. She never heard from or saw him again.

27

"FRATERNITY PRANK"
(A Man's Story)

The fraternity president and his girlfriend finally broke up after a few years of dating, due to irreconcilable differences. His now ex-girlfriend was on the prowl throughout the fraternity to get him back, as he was known for his infidelity on campus. Turned out, she was the daughter of a famous celebrity, one we are not allowed to mention as this book remains anonymous for obvious reasons. The fraternity held a huge bash at the house that upcoming Friday night, and she had planned to be there!

She was dressed in red so her now ex-boyfriend would surely see her, and that the other brothers would remember seeing her, in the hope of possibly taking one of them home. As she approached this one fellow in particular, she expressed her desires and intentions, in the form of a whisper in his right ear, bringing an immediate smile to his demeanor. With the lick of her lips, she whisked him away, grabbing his hand and leading him out to the parking lot. "Come on, lets go to my house", she cooed as she blew kisses to him trying to convince him to leave. "I think we should get a hotel room" he convinced her as he walked briskly toward his car and took control of the matter.

Being from the South, the fellow opened the girl's car door for her, allowing her to sit and then shut the door. Chivalrous in his behavior, he then walked intently toward his door and started the car. She sat on the other side, almost in tears as her ex-boyfriend never made gentlemanly gestures such as this. "What?" he asked as if to wonder what movie was playing in her head. She just sat and smiled as her hand and long, groomed fingers inched their way up his right thigh. He punched the gas, and they were off toward the Holiday Inn. As they checked in, the clerk at the front desk smirked and said, "Have a nice evening" and within minutes, they approached the hotel room door. The key offered the usual struggle, as all hotel rooms do, and then they were in the room giggling.

She immediately began kissing him passionately while trying to undress him. "Hey, hold on a second, give me a minute here" he said with his hand up as if to tell her to stop moving so fast. As she held off he then began kissing her, even more intently than her previous performance, and was fondling her breasts through her shirt. He slowly took off her top in one erotic movement. Systematically, he removed her bra, then her skirt, and then, "knock, knock, knock" on the door. "Oh my gosh, who could that be?" he said as he approached the keyhole on the door. Looking through the distorted lens, he saw a fraternity brother. "Do you think we should open the door?" she asked in a panic. "It will only be a second, I promise", he responded, and slid through a crack in the barely opened door. Just as he did, the door flew open, the fraternity brother entered yelling, "You slut, you are sooooo busted"! Humiliated, she jumped up, throwing on her clothes and the guy who drove her said, "We were only holding hands, really", as he winked at his fraternity brother. Turned out that the two guys planned this event to set up her up! Evidently, all the Greeks knew her plan for the evening, and some of them conspired together to help protect their fraternity president. The girl was told to get into the other fraternity brother's car, and she was taken back to the party to face up to this situation in front of her ex-boyfriend. The fellow went back to the party as well, but stopped by a bar on the way first, to allow for the coast to be cleared, for the two "ex's" had some sorting out to do. After returning to the fraternity party, he was handed a bottled beer, as opposed to the usual keg glass, and they toasted him with the fraternity chant. The ex-girlfriend left humiliated, never to show her face around his fraternity again for the rest of the year.

28

"LIMP EXIT"
(A Woman's Story)

It was January and two days after her official birthday, when she received the phone call. She had attended a seminar out of town earlier that day, and was driving back to town when he phoned to invite her to join him at the symphony later that evening, as a belated birthday present. The production was nicknamed "The Silver Rose" and she became excited about her date, hurrying home to look ultra fabulous for an evening she would never forget! The sky had been overcast on her drive back to Atlanta, and she was sure it would rain later that evening, so she dressed appropriately for the occasion and the weather. Either way, she was wearing her favorite red dress.

As he was approaching her home, he gave her a courtesy call, mentioning he was five minutes away and that he had a limp. "A limp?" she questioned. "Yeah, I was working out with my trainer the other night and he kept pushing me on squats, which in turn injured my knee", he responded in a cavalier tone. Without realizing it, she replied, "Why didn't you tell your trainer he was hurting you, I mean, didn't you know it was hurting your ligaments?" Embarrassed, but now in her driveway, he said, "I'll tell you all about it in a minute, I'm here." Laughing, but a little miffed at her injured date, she greeted him at the front door with a kiss and immediately wanted to know all about the workout the night before. It had started sprinkling outside, so he had an umbrella ready for her, which was both romantic and considerate. So far so good, she thought, except for his limping. Within two minutes, he proceeded to offer all the juicy details of his workout, how he found his trainer, which body parts he preferred to train harder on, and why he didn't tell his trainer to stop pushing him as hard as he does. She found the fact that he liked using and needed a personal trainer to get the benefits of a hot body truly disturbing. Most of her guy friends or ex-boyfriends all worked out with their friends, not paying someone to train them. Bored and unimpressed, she looked out the passenger window, trying to look for the side road which led to the elusive symphony parking garage. His story seemed to go on and on, all the while they drove in circles trying to find the garage, but amazingly by the third circle, they found it. Her anticipation of a fantastic production overwhelmed her and she reached for his hand, offering a comforting smile, lame date or not.

Limping as he exited his SUV, she wondered if he would survive walking up the stairs to the main level, down the hall, and sitting through a two hour production without getting gangrene in his leg! Upon entering the building, she made a mad dash towards the beverage cart, as if to say, "I'm going to need a drink!" He graciously bought her a glass of wine, but mentioned he couldn't join her in the celebration, as he had just taken another OxyContin, and it would not mesh well with the pain relief that he so desperately needed and keep him awake to enjoy the evening. She suggested he drink a whole lot of wine and call it a night, but the joke didn't take. Fortunately for him, they had several well organized and nice dates before this evening, so she was willing to let his issues slide for the moment. Unconvinced of his state, she genuinely inquired, "Are you ok, I mean, are you sure you want to go since you are in so much pain? I would rather not go in at all than to leave the symphony early and miss the ending." Her questioning only seemed to inflame the issue, as his medication was not adequate for his injury and his demeanor grew grumpy. He reassured her, "No, no, it's no big deal, really, I'll be fine. Let's just go in because I don't want to be lame". She shot him the, "Okay, but I'm warning you" look as he playfully slapped her ass. Moments later, an old friend walked up to her and said, "Hey, how have you been, it's been a long time?" Not recalling his name, she simply replied, "Yes, it has been a long time and it's great to see you". Her date grew both jealous and impatient, as the curtain call chimed for the crowd to start moving toward the doors for the show to begin. His pathetic limp made him look old, and his grumpiness portrayed him intolerable. She had grown tired of trying to make regular conversation, as he kept reminding her of how badly his knee was hurting, yet he was not willing to admit he should not have gone out that evening. "Pride will get you no where except in trouble", she thought, as they found their seats and the lights dimmed.

The Symphony was absolutely gorgeous and the guest opera singers were mesmerizing. The music made her dance in her seat, creating a special moment for the two of them. Just as she was tearing up from the beautiful opera singers professing their undying love for one another, he leaned over and said, "We have to go, I can't take the pain anymore". Disappointed but understanding, she said reluctantly, "Okay, if we must leave because you are in too much pain to stick it out until the end, then let's at least leave at the end of the scene, so not to disturb the other guests". "No, I have to leave right now, I can't wait!", he whined loud enough for the people two rows up to turn around and give him the "shhhhh" sign. She agreed to leave and waited for him to get up first as he was closer to the aisle. Once outside of the auditorium, she stated, "I knew this was going to happen, and to be quite frank, I'm not very happy about it either."

Lagging behind her, he sensed she was upset as she walked ahead of him, bitter of having to leave and getting wet from the rain, and irritated about her lame birthday present. Ashamed, he asked her to help him walk because it was unbearable for him to place any weight on his leg. They seemed to walk aimlessly as she forgot how to get back to the parking garage, and he was in too much pain to direct them. Just as things couldn't be worse, the rain fell hard, drenching her faux fur wrap, red silk gown, and her satin silver pumps and clutch, as he also forgot to grab the umbrella from his car. At this point, she was completely pissed, not knowing if she had the right to be upset because she didn't get to see the end of the symphony or feel sorry for her date. Either way, she had to drive his SUV back to her house, and have him come inside, place ice on his knee for an hour before allowing him to get behind the wheel and drive himself home. She even invited him to stay the night, for fear he might not make the thirty minute drive safely, but he refused saying he just wanted to be in his own surroundings and go to bed. The next day, she called to check on him, but could only leave a message. He never returned her phone call. Finally, after a week of leaving messages, she sent him a not-so-nice email requesting a courtesy reply as she was concerned for his safety. He eventually emailed her back, saying "I have been on pain medication for a week, and didn't even know which day it was, let alone, if my phone was ringing". His explanation was insufficient for her level of concern, so she sent him a simple email response, "Please, never use my phone number or email address again". Out of disgust for his inability to know "When to say when" in any situation, she decided he was not the man for her. They never spoke or saw one another again.

29

"AWKWARD SEPARATION" (A Man's Story)

A man and his wife were married for two years and began having problems. After the endless arguments and long nights of fighting, the wife decided to move out. A few weeks later, the man grew bored and went out for a drink, upon which he met a lovely lady. The lady was also going through a separation, which in a strange way became a comfort to the man, as he felt alienated from the rest of the people in the bar. They talked and drank, and talked and drank, and after becoming quite drunk he asked her if she wanted to go back to his house for yet another drink. She obliged to his offer, since she lived near Piedmont Park and they were in Marietta. Upon entering his home, he realized that the time was half past one o'clock in the morning, and decided that one more drink would do the trick before going to bed. He sat out on the couch with his new friend, flirting and bashing his soon-to-be-ex wife for about thirty minutes. She was yawning, probably due to his ongoing drawl of wife bashing, and motioned toward the bedroom, as if to hint to another more interesting topic. He picked up on the hint and said in a very insinuating manner,

"Oh, you want to go to bed, huh". They both laughed, as he collected the dirty stemware and headed towards the bedroom. He then simultaneously turned to smile at her, while he was turning the knob to the bedroom door, and realized in horror that his wife was sleeping on the bed. She woke up and yelled, "What are you doing?" Gasping for words and equally surprised he just shut the door out of embarrassment. He turned to the young lady and said, "We've got to go", and they got a hotel room. By now, it was about three o'clock in the morning when stress of the previous scenario and mere exhaustion took over. They just slept and snuggled, which evidentially did not amuse the young lady, as she presumed a sexual encounter. The next morning, the young lady was becoming wacky in her behavior and he was desperate to take her home. After driving her home to Midtown, which took nearly an hour, he thought to himself, "I just went from one crazy woman to the next!" He never asked her for her phone number and switched watering holes.

30

"Shirt Art"
(A Woman's Story)

She had been infatuated with him for about a year now when he finally noticed her. He invited her to his house in Brookhaven, which was a thirty minute drive from her home in Roswell. He had planned to take her on a motorcycle ride through the park to pick flowers, which she thought was very romantic. As the wind blew on her face and her hair became slightly messy, she envisioned herself on the back of his motorcycle again, and she began to smile. As they neared his home, she jumped off his motorcycle and into her SUV to check herself in the mirror, and then followed him into his home. He directed her into the kitchen for a glass of wine and amuse-bouche, a sort of mouth teaser to excite her palate for an amazing dinner to come. She took notice of his attention to detail on every aspect of the evening, as if to amuse and entice her. She was hooked, line, and sinker.

A lovely dinner was prepared, comprising of duck confit, couscous and creamed spinach, which posed a very delightful surprise, as she had no idea that he possessed such exceptional talent in the kitchen, leaving her truly impressed. Speechless, he led her into the family room, where he proceeded to indulge in a fine conversation about his first automobile, and how the gem of a car had been wrecked by a former girlfriend. She grew weary of hearing him go on and on, and decided to be bold and silence him with a kiss, which seemed to be a successful move. The room grew very quiet, except for the occasional smacking sounds of rolling tongues and lips meeting. She was a little embarrassed, so she pulled away to meet his eyes with hers, only encouraging him to ravage her completely. Right there on the couch, they engaged in a full-on make-out session, not caring who might walk in the front door, as his neighbors tended to make themselves at home unpredictably.

His hands did all the walking, and unbuttoning, and removing of most of her clothes, even his own, which turned her on even more. With only their undergarments remaining, adding to the sensuality of the moment, she moved towards him as if to imply her certain intentions. He immediately caught onto her motive and with one fine swoop, he was naked, placing his hand on the back of her head, and directing her mouth towards his penis. She had to brace herself because he was more than above average, this man, she realized, would have made millions in the porn industry! Normally, she loved performing oral sex for a man, but this was actual work, as he barely fit inside her mouth. Realizing he appreciated her efforts for about fifteen minutes, she noticed he was nearing an orgasm so she pulled away to say, "Please let me know when you are about to orgasm, because I don't want you to cum inside my mouth". Surprised that she stopped and was talking, he replied, "Yeah, yeah, okay, whatever, just don't stop what you're doing, I'm almost there", he said almost rushing her so the feeling would not subside. Five minutes later, he announced the arrival with "Okay", loud enough for the neighbors to hear, and she pulled her mouth away from his penis, just in time for him to grab the base of his cock and move it in the fastest helicopter motion she had ever witnessed, causing her to squint from airborne orgasmic matter. This created a form of cum art on her shirt. He thought he had removed her shirt, but at some point she had put it back on, not knowing if his roommate would enter the house unexpectedly, and she would be undressed in the room. He was overwhelmed with bliss as he drifted away on the couch with a smile. Meanwhile, she sat there on the floor, covered with a spin art design on her very expensive, dry clean only silk shirt. Upset, she stormed into the hallway bathroom, which he only slightly noticed the tone in her voice when she questioned sarcastically "Was that good for you?"

"Are you okay", he asked in a cavalier tone. "What do you think, you jerk", she retorted, as she stepped into the light enough for him to see only a faint residue of his orgasm on her blouse. "Oh damn, did I do that?" he asked sleepily and really not caring. She just gave him a look as if to say, "You think?!" He could sense that she was upset but took the typical "She will get over it" attitude, and let her leave in a storm of rage. He tried calling her an hour after she left, not realizing that she would have to do the walk of shame into her own home now, with her child's babysitter to be paid, and sent home. His audacity was infuriating, as the perfect image she held for him had now changed into a disrespectful, bastard one. Fuming, she noticed that she still had his motorcycle helmet in her car, as she set it on her seat while she fluffed her hair after their ride. Her thoughts turned to "getting even" by selling the helmet on Ebay. At least she could get dry cleaning money.

31

"TROUBLE WITH THE TEACHER"
(A Man's Story)

A Project Manager guy met an Elementary School Teacher girl out at a bar one weekend, and after some extensive flirting, they exchanged phone numbers. Later in the week, they connected and agreed to meet back at the same area to eat at a popular sushi restaurant. Once they arrived, he noticed how much prettier she was without his beer goggles from the previous weekend, so he anticipated an amazing evening of getting to know one another. Conversation went well and the sushi was satisfying, so he ordered a large, hot sake to share. A little buzzed from the sake, he suggested they continue their evening at the nearby bar, upon which they originally had met. Smiling and blushing, she agreed it would be a good idea, and he reached to hold her hand, knowing it was going to be a memorable evening.

The bar was packed and they both knew several people once inside, so they settled for barstools at the back bar, and started doing shots. It was three shots down when they realized it was now one o'clock in the morning. "I really need to let my dog out or he will definitely have an accident", she slurred drunkenly. He agreed but knew she would never find her way out of the crazy road maze that led them to the bar, so he drove his car in front of hers to lead the way. After the third turn to the right, her Volkswagen Bug hopped the curb, and the police car that trailed them pulled her over. The officer issued a sobriety test upon which she failed miserably while vomiting by the back wheel of her car. "What am I going to do now", she said through tears. "I guess you will be going to jail but I will wait for you. Let me see what I can do", he reassured her as the police officer placed handcuffs on her wrists and put her in the backseat. He watched her as she looked sadly at him, while the police car disappeared towards the county jail.

He had never been in this position before and was unsure of what to do so he chose the first thing that came to mind: Bail Bondsman. The problem was that he didn't know how much to pay for her release, so he followed the police car to the jail to inquire about the bail bond. The smart ass lady at the front responded, "For Ms. Johnson, that will be five hundred dollars for her release, and she has to stay over night until she sobers up, it's the law". Frustrated and irritated, and completely sober at this point, he drove to the nearest open bail bonds facility. Upon entering, he saw big signs stating "Cash only, No Checks" and he looked at the guy at the counter and said, "I will be back with cash", as if that guy had never heard that statement before. After hitting up the Bank of America's ATM five miles away, he made his way back to the bail bonds facility and paid her bail, received his receipt for the transaction, then left tired and exhausted. "I'm working way too hard for this girl, damn", he mustered in a low, weak tone. As he re-entered the jail, he was frankly informed by the lovely greeter that he would have to wait outside for Ms. Johnson until after her release. "We will let her know that you have paid her bail and that you are outside in your car, that's what everyone has to do", she told him. "That's the law", he mumbled to himself as he walked back outside to his car and fell asleep. The time was now seven o'clock in the morning when she finally knocked on his car door, reeking of jail smells, and he drove her back to her car that was conveniently parked on the curb just blocks away from the bar.

Once they neared her Volkswagen, he noticed that the tire that jumped the curb was flat, and then they discovered that she did not have a tire iron, neither did he. Stuck, he flagged down a guy in a van who kindly assisted in changing her flat tire. Jumping into their own cars, they headed full speed to her apartment to let the damn dog out, knowing full well that he had left a few presents for her to clean up. They walked in, grabbed the dog and leash, and relieved the dog of pressures, then headed back inside. All the while, they laughed about the evening, of what happened to her inside jail and what he had to deal with outside of jail. Once the ice was broken, they began making out heavily, despite the jail stench on her hair, skin and clothes. They made their way into her bedroom, both anticipating the finale of the evening. Simultaneously, he started to undo her bra and noticed an empty condom wrapper on her bedside table! Disgusted, he froze up and stopped kissing her. He didn't know what to say and didn't want to embarrass her, but knew he also didn't want to go any further with her since there wasn't exactly a date on the opening of the wrapper. Feeling strange, he left the apartment reasoning he was too tired to continue. He never called her again, and didn't answer any other numerous phone calls she had left for him. He should have realized that once she was hauled off to jail that he should have seen the neon, blinking, warning sign reading, "Five hundred dollars down the drain, and no, you are NOT getting laid".

32

"Bottom of the Barrel"
(A Woman's Story)

A girl goes to Skybar in Hollywood and is sitting down with a group of friends drinking a cocktail. In mid-sentence to one of her friends, a rock star patron approaches her, interrupting, "You're hot!" Smiling, she recognizes the rock star and replied, "Why thank you". They talked for a while until screaming sentences grew tiresome, so they left to head to his house.

In the car, he lays on the charm by telling her he has rock star drugs at his house, and enough liquor to pimp a whore house, believing she is impressed. At this point, the liquor was setting in as she grew nauseated from his whipping around the hillside in his Porsche. Once she spotted his yellow and crooked teeth in real lighting in his home, her nausea worsened.

She entered his home and settled down on the couch, as he proceeded to set the mood by lighting candles, and pulling down elegant glasses and pouring them both a glass of champagne. The music was hypnotic, a Karma Sutra type genre, which moved her and created a nice groove. The moment was elemental as he was priming his prey. As she sipped from her champagne, she was overwhelmed by nausea, and projectile vomited toward the fireplace.

Appalled and embarrassed for her, the rock star immediately jumped up from the couch, and ran into the kitchen to grab a towel to clean up the mess. He commented, "Whoa girl, damn, that was some crazy shit! You want to slip into something more comfortable?" His words weren't coming out clear to her as she felt her head spin and ache, and she projectile vomited again, this time she aimed at the staircase, parallel to the couch. "Oh my god, girl", he exclaimed in his British accent. "What the hell is wrong with me, I was fine a moment ago? I think it was your driving that made me ill", she blamed as she felt sick again. This time, her nausea allowed her some time to make it to the bathroom, and she laid by the porcelain god for at least an hour after that. He occasionally visited her, rubbing her back, and then trying to grab her ass or her breasts. Annoyed, she told him to give her some time to feel better, but she never fully recovered.

The next morning, she awoke in front of the toilet and staggered out into the living room, which proved her prior illness. The room looked like it needed to be scrubbed down, as the tan carpet and white walls were inked in red, evident of strawberry daiquiri and calamari consumption the previous evening. Disgusted and hung over, she found the rock star passed out upstairs in his bedroom. He was completely naked, and she had to beg him to get dressed in order to go back to the club where her car was parked. Irritable and put out because he did not get the sex he was hoping for, he slung on a pair of jeans without underwear, threw on a t-shirt and flip flops and said, "Come on, girl, let's get you out of here". Once the hangover cloud cleared, she assumed, as did her friends, that someone had put a mickie in her drink, as her immediate nausea was uncommon. He never apologized or offered to contact her, or even obtain her phone number. Sadly, the rock star did not appear as statuesque as she had imagined. In her eyes, he was the bottom of the barrel.

33

"Jail Birds"
(A Woman's Story)

A woman gets set up on a blind date by a friend and she meets him at Dantanna's by Lenox Mall. He was a 6'2", southern, handsome man, and she was grateful for his presence. With a smile he asked, "What do you want to drink"? She suggests chardonnay, but he orders "the merlot" mispronouncing the wine with a "t" at the end. Not knowing if she heard him correctly, she gave him a smile and said, "What did you just say?" He repeated the type of wine and again saying the "t" at the end, and combined with his southern drawl, it just sounded terrible! Embarrassed, she replied, "That sounds nice". The server brought the bottle of wine, opened the bottle and presented her with the sample of wine. She tasted it, and almost cringed due to the cheapness of the wine, then suffered through the first twenty minutes of the dining experience due to loud sounds of the basketball game playing in the other room. "Why did he choose a sports bar for our first date?" she thought to herself over and over again until the server approached them to take their dinner order.

After dinner and a bottle of "Merrr-lott" later, they decided to go to Beluga Martini Bar for drinks and live jazz music. His phone rang and he said he would be right back. She sat at the bar waiting patiently for his return but he never came back. Perplexed and humiliated, she drove her car to Beluga, thinking he might have become mixed up and decided to drive there. Upon arriving, she asked the valet if he had come by and they confirmed he had not. She decided to go inside anyway and order a drink, as she needed to keep her buzz going if this date would be continuing. Glancing down at her watch, she realized that it was now eleven o'clock in the evening. Then her cell phone rang. It was her daughter, crying and desperately trying to form words that she was in jail for a hit and run incident earlier on in the evening. Now upset, the woman jumped off the barstool and headed for the valet to get to her car. She reassured her daughter that she was going to drive to the Fulton County jail to bail her out then hung up the phone. Just as she was about to leave, she decided to phone her friend who had set her up on the date and told her the events of the evening. With disbelief, the friend apologized profusely for the error of the choice of date she had made for her friend. "That's okay, I just wished he could have not left me hanging around at the bar. I felt that was just rude", she said almost in tears of the embarrassment of being disliked by the man.

The woman managed to pick up her daughter from jail, paid the heavy fines, sign where needed, then proceeded to her home. She took a shower, began to cry and eventually fell asleep. The next morning, the friend who had set her up on the date phoned her with an explanation. "Girl, you are not going to believe this, but he was in jail!" "What?!" the woman said in a loud, disbelieving tone. "What happened?" The friend then told her all about how he had taken a phone call and sat in his car while it was running, as a police officer drove up beside him and asked him to roll down his window. The guy had refused, and was motioning at the officer in a rude and crass manner. The officer exited his car, approached the man who was talking on his phone, and rapped on the window. The man then flew open his car door, almost hitting the officer, and staggered out of the car in a very drunken manner. The officer asked him if he had been drinking and he denied the question. Then the officer told him he had to do a sobriety test and the man failed the test, blowing way beyond the limit to drive. The officer then placed the man in the back seat of the police car and then he turned off the man's car, giving him his keys. He was taken to Fulton County jail, same place as the woman's daughter, and was left there until morning. He had just been released from jail and phoned the lady who had set them up, to explain his disappearance. Stunned, the woman sat in silence. She couldn't believe that in one night both her date and daughter had been in the same jail at the same time, realizing they were more of a match than she initially thought. He was too embarrassed to phone her though, so they never saw one another again.

34

"SMELLY DATE"
(A Man's Story)

A guy met up with a girl that he had previously had sex with. After a bottle of red wine, they became very drunk. She invited him back to her house, and upon entering he noticed that everything, wall to wall, was white. Her couch became quite comfy, as they immediately began making out on the chaise lounger. Within ten minutes, she encouraged him to follow her into her bedroom. She led him down the white carpeted hallway to her bedroom, removing her tank top in a whirl and wrapping it around his neck. He accomplished what he was brought back to her room to accomplish, and got up to get a glass of water from the kitchen. Excited to find a half-drunken bottle of red wine, he poured himself a glass. Before finishing the glass, he was overwhelmed with the need to break wind, not realizing that he had just defecated himself. He then went back to her bedroom, and proceeded to wake her enough to begin making love to her again. As he approached climax, he thought he had to break wind again but, instead, defecated himself again, sensing it this time enough to cause him to jump up out of bed and head to the bathroom. Too drunk to notice if he got all the mess off, he went back to her bed, leaving his messy jeans and boxers on the floor, and resumed the position with the girl until he passed out.

At six o'clock in the morning and a few hours of sleep later, he wakes and attempts to put on his boxers and jeans, but notices they were very slippery and he can't seem to figure out the reason. As he was struggling to pull his jeans on, he noticed the stench of poop, realizing that it was getting all over his legs, and he recalls getting up earlier when he thought he just farted. Mortified, he backed down the hallway and accidentally bumped into the big ashtray, spewing ashes all over the white carpet in the living room. Gasping, he freaked out once he put two and two together of the mess he made. By now, poop had dripped down onto his feet, getting all over the floor as he panicked to clean up the mess, only to exacerbate the issue. He hurried around the living room, bumping into the curtains and furniture, trying desperately to clean up the mess from every piece of furniture it seemed, even her white couch. Then he bolted from her apartment, leaving behind him a disaster. He called his friend to pick him up, but she didn't answer. Not sure of what else to do, he appeared unannounced at another friend's house to get a ride. Later on that day, the girl called one of their mutual friends and described the scene, not sure of the events that took place but simply stated, "It really smells bad in here!" She never heard from him again.

35
"Dirty Little Secrets"
(A Man's Story)

A Senior male in high school was spending quality time outside of school, in his basement after hours, with a fellow Senior female. She used to sneak out and stay with him until four o'clock in the morning, even on a school night, to have sex. Meanwhile, in daylight hours at school, the two hardly spoke because she was the most popular and beautiful cheerleader, dating the star quarterback of the football team.

One day, they decided to skip school and meet at her house to "go swimming". They went up to her room to "change" and it all started to get steamy. As the mirrors fogged, her Father came home early from work and heard noises upstairs, so he decided to investigate. In mid thrust, he opened the sliding bathroom door exposing them on the bathroom floor naked and engaged fully in sexual contact. Her Father's eyes met the boy's eyes, and the boy knew he was in real trouble. Naked, the boy bolted from the bathroom, leaving the girl naked and sprawled out on the floor. The boy ran from her house, down the street while his semi-erect penis swayed in the air. He flew into his house, ran past his Mother who obviously was very surprised as he yelled, "hhhheeeeeelllllpppp" to his Father who was sitting nearby. Two seconds later, the doorbell rang. The girl's Father was standing outside ready for action. The boy's Father opened the door and the girl's Father stated plainly, "Your son was just caught fornicating with my daughter". The boy's Father responded simply, "Sorry", and he slammed the door in the other Father's face. The boy let out a sigh of relief that night. Despite the embarrassment, the two continued their romantic affairs even into college years. As time went on they eventually drifted apart, but to his joy the girl did not marry the quarterback, and he never knew of her infidelity, keeping their dirty little secrets.

36

"Psycho Ex-Girlfriend"
(A Woman's Story)

A girl and her friends were invited to hang out at the Pike house fraternity party one Friday evening with one of the fraternity brothers. The evening was cruising along at normal party speed, music was cranked, and the keg full of cheap beer. The girls roamed around a little, checking out the scene, and having a good time flirting with the guys. Just then, the psycho ex-girlfriend appeared on the scene, alone and with contention for her ex-boyfriend, who happened to be the same guy the girl was hanging out with. The ex-girlfriend knew that the girl was invited there, and began following the ladies around, making sure there wasn't any funny business going on with her now ex-boyfriend. As the night grew older, the time had come for the party to end, and the new couple debated where they should sleep. "Let's just go to my room here at the house, it will be ok", he convinced her, saying good-bye to her girlfriends.

As they approached his room, he noticed that the door was cracked a little. His ex-girlfriend had been there, he knew it! And to their surprise, she was lying on his bed at that very moment, waiting for them. Her grimacing face and loud voice offered the perfect opportunity for them to leave, and head to his friend's house where they could be alone in his guest bedroom. Embarrassed for him, the girl leaned over to kiss his cheek to let him know that she understood his pain. As they approached the house, the ex-girlfriend ran at them from the bushes, and began hitting him with her handbag while yelling and screaming profanity. Realizing his friend was under attack, the guy who owned the house ran out onto the front lawn, grasping the house phone in his hand. The guy told the girl he was calling the police, and threatened her to leave or he would have her arrested for trespassing and harassment. The girl eventually left, as she heard police cars approaching his house.

The police arrived and asked the guy if he wanted to file a report against the girl for harassment, but he declined as he figured she would have learned her lesson, and not bother him again. As the guy retired to his room, and the police left the premises, the new couple went to the guest bedroom to sleep. There were no moves to make love or even kiss. They were mentally and emotionally drained, as the guy felt too embarrassed of his ex-girlfriend's behavior to be involved with anyone else until things subsided. The next day the guy offered, "I'll call you later" but she never heard from him again. Oh well, just goes to show that just because a guy says he broke up with his girlfriend doesn't mean she broke up with him!

37

"PREGNANCY BY OSMOSIS"
(A Man's Story)

A recently divorced male agreed to be his friend's wingman, as his friend had met a girl on Match dot com during the previous week, and he desperately wanted to meet her in person. The guys met the girl out at a local pub and once the introductions were made, the recently divorced male became intrigued with online dating. So, he signed up on the dating website, hoping to find Mrs. Wonderful and found there were many beautiful women on the site. Eventually, he found a pretty little maid himself! They exchanged phone numbers and agreed upon a future date.

Their first date was to meet up at an Oktoberfest party in Midtown, and it took a while to find one another due to the large crowd, but eventually they met. She was very intoxicated, slurring her words, stumbling around, and acted belligerent. Unsure if he should leave her in that condition, he stuck around to insure her safety, managing to get a few good sentences out of her. Her friends were talking to him more than she was, and if not for their presence, their first date would have been extremely awkward. Over the course of the evening, she kissed him, knowing he had to drive her home. Two days later, he met her at a pizza place, and decided he wanted to get to know her better. They ate, and drank, and laughed, and enjoyed one another's company. So much that she invited him back to her house for another cocktail. He turned down her offer, which made her upset enough to leave. Confused at her irrational behavior, he paid the tab and drove home, seriously believing he would never see her again, much to his error.

Several days later, she sent numerous text messages to his cell phone, so he decided to call her to get to the bottom of the madness. She invited him to meet her out for a drink and he agreed to meet her, this time having one eye open to her inability to hold her liquor and a conversation at the same time. Unknowing where the conversation would take him, he sat back and listened to her break up with him, from a relationship that never existed. She continued flatly, "I want out of this relationship or whatever it is that we are doing". He interrupted her to mention, "I am just taking things slow, besides I hardly even know you", which just exacerbated the issue. She chimed in with a slight shriek, "I don't want to move slowly, that's what you want. This is on you!" Confused at what was happening, he continued to sit and listen to her irrational antics, and eventually left after paying the bill, thinking he would never see the drama queen again.

His friend told him that on Match dot com, women usually feel desperate, and it often becomes addicting to "Find a Match", so he tried to be understanding of her behavior. A few weeks later, her birthday party was being held at a restaurant in the Highlands, and he was invited to attend. All afternoon she called and sent text messages to him, leaving obnoxious messages such as, "Why don't you answer your damn phone?!" He showed up at the restaurant where the party was being held, and her friends were being very loud, so he offered to buy her a drink at another bar.

She agreed and left with him, after just thirty minutes of his arrival. Just as predicted, she became very drunk, and began accusing him of being hung up on his ex-wife. Realizing how drunk and upset she was, and knowing he couldn't tolerate her any longer, he offered to get her a cab. He had created a monster at this point! Without warning, she then whirled around and round-kicked him in the chest, screaming obscenities in retort to his offer of a cab. Shocked at being kicked, he turned around and began walking the other direction, trying to separate himself from her. She proceeded to run after him, apologizing and admitting she had overreacted by kicking him. He accepted her apology, but continued to walk away and drove home, hoping he would not have to see her again.

That night, and for the following week, she constantly called him and sent text messages, but he never responded, hoping she would stop. The last text he received said, "It's yours", and he couldn't resist to call her. She stated very calmly, "It's yours, I just know it". He asked her, "Sweetheart, you are thirty years old. How do you think you could be pregnant by me if we haven't even had sex, by osmosis?" He hung up the phone, swearing he would never talk to her again. Unfortunately, he ran into her a year later at a block party, and she began sending text messages to him again asking, "Don't you want to buy me a drink?" Tempted by sarcasm, he suppressed his response, "Sure, I will buy you a drink, by osmosis!"

38
"MILLIONAIRE HANDS"
(A Woman's Story)

She met him on Millionaire Match dot com, and he claimed to be a wealthy dermatologist from Ft. Lauderdale, Florida. After several late night conversations online, and phone calls, the millionaire said he wanted to fly up to Atlanta to see her. Once his travel arrangements were finalized, he notified her of his reservations at the Hilton Hotel by the airport. She agreed to pick him up, and responded with a school girl giddiness, "Okay, see you tonight!"

Her sense of direction was never correct, and she was too busy talking to her friend on her cellular phone to remember where she was, so she just kept circling the Hartsfield Airport until he phoned in and interrupted her unimportant phone conversation. "Where are you? I'm getting hungry!" he asked impatiently. "I'm on my way", she responded in a slightly annoyed tone. "I just don't know where your hotel is, and I'm circling the airport trying to find it!" He huffed for a moment and said, "Hold on, I will get someone who lives here to find out where you are, and give you directions to the hotel". He located the concierge counter, and then phoned her back with a local person to assist her. She eventually made it to the front of the hotel, where he had been waiting for almost an hour past their agreed upon time. It was obvious to the both of them that the date was starting off on the wrong foot, so they greeted each other with a light kiss on the cheek and a hug and she said, "Shall we go eat dinner?" He nodded, suggesting they hit the hotel lounge where they were serving complimentary buffet, as a jazz trio played for the elderly guests. She gave him a questioning look, one that issued an obvious "Uh, no" response to his suggestion, and he laughed out loud. He awkwardly kissed her on top of her head, stating "You're beautiful", and then directed her to the lounge, where they ordered a drink from the bar. The whole time they were at the bar, he kept rubbing on her legs, and trying to look deep into her crystal blue eyes, which was creeping her out. Then he stated out of nowhere, "Okay let's go out, I was just testing you" and requested the tab from the bartender. He was the only one laughing. They walked to valet and she realized, as they waited for her car, that he had placed his hand on the small of her back, rubbing his hand in a strange circular motion. She thought that was weird, but didn't ask him to remove his hand, believing he would eventually stop.

Once in her car, she decided to call up her girlfriend who had suggested a restaurant that might be fun on a Friday night, despite her poor planning. Again, she noticed his hand, only this time he had moved it to her right thigh, and he was rubbing up and down her leg. Almost as soon as she was about to say something to him, her friend answered, "Hey girl" with an enthusiastic southern drawl. "Hey, what was the name of that restaurant you mentioned earlier, and how do we get there from the airport", she questioned her friend, as her octopus-hands date sat beside her clueless and option-less of what to do that evening. Her friend issued directions and wished them well on their date, as they hurried to the restaurant. Once they arrived at Eclipse de Luna, the woman eagerly jumped out of her SUV, and simultaneously out of the clutches of her date, announcing, "I could use a drink right about now", but he did not respond. "Funny", she thought to herself, "But usually guys would have chimed right in with that comment. Huh." She decided to let him take the lead, and they entered the front doors, upon which they were greeted by the hostess, "Good Evening and welcome to Eclipse de Luna! We have a cover charge tonight of twenty dollars". The girl replied, "What's going on tonight for a cover charge?" The hostess responded, "It's a 99-X Radio event with special giveaways all night and drink specials too." The woman smiled at her date, hoping he would still want to go inside, and he reluctantly paid the cover charges. She approached the bar and ordered a glass of wine, and while searching for her credit card, she discovered the sign above the bar that plainly stated, "Cash only transactions". Embarrassed but desperate for a drink, she turned to her date, who was now across the room hanging out with the hostess at the front of the restaurant. Frustrated, she walked up to him and said in the most polite manner possible, "Would you please buy my glass of wine, I have my credit card but they only accept cash here". He gave her a puzzled look and then responded with a huff, "Okay, but I don't think I like this place, it seems cheesy". She was realizing that it was her date that was cheesy. After paying for her drink, he walked to the other side of the bar, trying to avoid her as his dramatic mood swing now had affected their chemistry. She stood by the bar for a moment, analyzing his physique, noticing his petite frame and balding head. It was evident that he had posted a younger version of himself on the website, and that they needed to bring this date to a close. She approached him saying, "I have a long day tomorrow and a long drive ahead of me, so do you mind if I take you back to the hotel?" He agreed stating flatly, "I didn't like this place anyway". On the way back to his hotel, her date acted like he was going to become sick, and ordered her to pull over. He walked slowly around the car about ten times, as nausea consumed him. She was relieved when they approached the hotel, and she gladly said, "Goodnight" with a courtesy, "Nice to meet you". He smiled and gave her a hug, as she made a beeline for the hotel lounge for a much needed cocktail. She stayed there two hours when she realized she needed to get home to let her dogs out, so she paid her tab and made her way out to her car.

Once inside her car, she realized she did not know how to get back to the highway, and became lost driving up and down the frontage roads from the hotel. Not long after, she was pulled over by a police officer who noticed her swerving from lane to lane. He issued her a ticket for reckless driving and, luckily, she escaped a sobriety test on one condition: that she contact a friend or family member to pick her up or she would go to jail for drunk driving. And there she sat, until the only person who picked up their phone at three o'clock in the morning was the manager of the local smoothie store. He kindly agreed to rescue her and pick her up. Relieved and tired of the eventful evening, she climbed into her friend's car and he took her home. The next day she stayed in with the covers over her head, barely making it out to take the dogs for a potty break. "What a nightmare date", she mustered under her breath, as she canceled her Millionaire Match account.

39
"MAMA DRAMA"
(A Man's Story)

A total sucker for strippers was introduced to a gorgeous Polish woman by one of his longtime girlfriends. Turned out the pair were equally interested in one another, so they exchanged phone numbers and agreed to a date. Little did he know what he was getting himself into in the next few weeks.

The raving idiot called the self-centered bitch the next day to ask her out and planned an outrageously expensive dinner date in hopes to get her in the sack, truth be told, in which she gladly accepted the dinner invitation. He suggested a popular seafood restaurant, and they had a great time mulling over steamed shrimp and their previously heinous dates and relationships, seeking pleasure in one another's disastrous dating debacles. The date had gone so well they decided to go on several other dinner dates, mainly because he obviously didn't get laid that night. Inevitably, he was introduced to her nightmare of a five-year-old son. Turned out, the blind idiot became very turned on to the fact that the slut was a Mother, not shy to show affection and love to her bratty son, sure to be a classic Oedipus complex situation, which he would have never predicted or maybe he just chose to ignore the obvious. Her bastard son was being a royal pain in the neck, and continued to be a thorn in his side throughout the evening. The woman did not discipline her son nor did she address the issue of his ill behavior during dinner, so the guy felt like he needed to take control and say something due to the growing audience surrounding their table. Fortunately for the whiny child, the enabling Mother wanted to leave, so he paid the tab and drove them home.

The following week, the infamous Grandmother (Mother of enabler) was in town and they invited the idiot to join them at a nearby Mexican restaurant. The total sucker ensured a timely arrival in hopes of impressing both his date and her Mother with his promptness. It isn't obvious that he wanted to get laid, is it? His punctuality worked and the guy and Grandmother hit it off! Within fifteen minutes of his arrival, the bastard child had not received his drink (it was covered up with electric blue tassels), so he began pulling on his Grandmother's shirt (she wore black tassels) in order to get a soda from her. The Grandmother struggled, keeping her shirt on, thank God, and was trying to settle the boy down, but he continued to misbehave. Benadryl anyone? Luckily, the waitress arrived and, overhearing the little boy, she brought him a soda. The remainder of the evening was consumed with exclamations of, "Mom!" and "Son, I said stop it!" The ball-less guy grew tired of the Mommy Act and eventually left, driving home in a frustrated daze, contemplating if calling to spend time with her again would be worth his while. And then he remembered that her birthday was coming up the following Monday, so he had to hurry home to look up a florist to deliver her flowers.

Embarrassingly true. The sucker called her the day of her birthday to wish her "Happy Birthday", but she made no mention of the delivered floral gift. Then he called the day after her birthday and asked, "Where would you like to go for your birthday dinner?", as they had planned to dine that Wednesday due to family being in town. She replied, "My birthday was yesterday. Why did you send me flowers today?" Shocked at her lack of appreciation to his gift, he defended, "The florist said they were slammed and would deliver them as soon as possible, I mean, I did order them on Sunday to be delivered Monday!" Not knowing what else to say, he tried to blow it off, continuing to make dinner plans. At the end of the phone conversation he recalled their evening at a strip club, which she suggested they go to, and her strange behavior and request while at the club. She asked in a childlike voice, "Do I get a tiara for my birthday?" He questioned, "A tiara?" She confirmed, "Yes, a tiara, to wear during dinner". "Sure", he responded, not knowing why she would ask for such a strange gift and where he would possibly find one on such short notice. He hung up and immediately phoned their mutual friend for advice. The conversation they had quickly summed up all his questions: she was a former stripper, who was accustomed to making a lot of money, having very extravagant birthdays, and was therefore spoiled rotten. He hung up and began preparing for the worst, as he phoned the restaurant and made reservations for her birthday dinner.

He promptly picked her up the next day and she looked stunning as always. They drove to the restaurant to make the reservation at seven o'clock in the evening. Everything was going well during dinner, except at the end, she began asking for her tiara in a childlike voice again. He said he couldn't find one and apologized. Disappointed, she began pouting and making strange whimpering sounds. Embarrassed of his date's behavior, he tried to console her. Realizing she was impossible to please, he grew to be disgusted as her behavior resembled that of her son. He hurried through the remainder of dinner, hoping she could pull it together enough to stop pouting and finish her meal, or at least appreciate it. After paying the tab, he drove her home and got no action from her, which really inflamed the issue. He decided then and there not to accept her phone calls after that night and wrote her off, chalking it up as another good date gone bad. Like Mother like Son.

40

"MR. WEIRDO"
(A Woman's Story)

A woman was set up on a blind date with the friend of a friend's roommate, and they agreed to meet at the local movie theater. He offered to pick her up at 7pm mentioning, "The movie begins at 7:30pm so there will not be time to eat dinner". It was a strange beginning to a date, but she figured that the less time she committed to this stranger the better as anything could go wrong.

Upon arriving at the theater, he approached the concession counter and ordered an extra large popcorn, large soda, and milk duds, but didn't offer her anything. She decided she didn't want anything, as she assumed she could snack on his pile of food. She was sadly mistaken, as he engulfed the soda midway through the movie, munching his popcorn so loudly it was difficult for her to hear the punch lines. Despite the fact that it was a guy action movie, the actual comedy of the movie became her struggle to hear the movie through his munching. At the end of the movie, he refilled his popcorn and soda, taking them with him as they left the theater. Mortified, she walked a little behind him as he clicked for the alarm on his car to go off then to unlock the doors. "Finally, something chivalrous that he will open my car door", she thought to herself. Much to her surprise, he opened the back door to strap in his beloved popcorn and soda, murmuring to himself, "I don't want them to spill". "Really? You didn't just do that!" she heard herself say a little louder than she had planned, and he gave her a look like, "What?" Funny, but the popcorn and soda did not spill on their way to take her home. Oh, how sweet that was. She never heard from him again and even if she had, she would have never consented to another date with the weirdo.